Assemblage Theory and Method

ALSO AVAILABLE AT BLOOMSBURY

Deleuze, Guattari, and the Problem of Transdisciplinarity,
Guillaume Collett
Deleuze and Guattari: Selected Writings, Kenneth Surin
Deleuze and Guattari's 'Anti-Oedipus': A Reader's Guide, Ian Buchanan

Schizoanalytic Applications series
Series editors: Ian Buchanan, David Savat, and Marcelo Svirsky

Titles include:
Deleuze and the Schizoanalysis of Feminism,
edited by Janae Sholtz and Cheri Lynne Carr
Deleuze and the Schizoanalysis of Religion,
edited by Lindsay Powell-Jones and F. LeRon Shults
Deleuze and the Schizoanalysis of Literature,
edited by Ian Buchanan, Tim Matts and Aidan Tynan

Deleuze Encounters series
Series editor: Ian Buchanan
Titles include:

Cinema After Deleuze, Richard Rushton
Philosophy After Deleuze, Joe Hughes

Assemblage Theory and Method

Ian Buchanan

BLOOMSBURY ACADEMIC

LONDON • NEW YORK • OXFORD • NEW DELHI • SYDNEY

BLOOMSBURY ACADEMIC
Bloomsbury Publishing Plc
50 Bedford Square, London, WC1B 3DP, UK
1385 Broadway, New York, NY 10018, USA

BLOOMSBURY, BLOOMSBURY ACADEMIC and the Diana logo are trademarks of
Bloomsbury Publishing Plc

First published in Great Britain 2021
Reprinted 2021

A catalogue record for this book is available from the British Library.

Library of Congress Cataloging-in-Publication Data
Names: Buchanan, Ian, 1969- author.
Title: Assemblage theory and method : an introduction and guide / Ian Buchanan.
Description: London ; New York : Bloomsbury Academic, 2021. | Includes bibliographical
references and index. | Summary: "What do we mean when we talk of an 'assemblage'
in contemporary theory? Any and every thing, or more precisely, any and every kind of
collection of things, could now be called an assemblage. The constant and seemingly
limitless expansion of the term's range of applications begs the question, if any and every
kind of collection of things is an assemblage, then what advantage is there is in using this
term and not some other term, or indeed no term at all? What makes an assemblage an
assemblage, and not some other kind of collection of things? This book advances beyond
this impasse and offers practical help in thinking about and using assemblage theory
for contemporary cultural and social research, in order to: – Answer the question: what
is assemblage theory? – Explain why assemblage theory is necessary – Provide clear
instructions on how to use assemblage theory The first book of it's kind, Ian Buchanan's guide
maps the beginnings of a brand new field within the humanities"–Provided by publisher.
Identifiers: LCCN 2020019590 (print) | LCCN 2020019591 (ebook) | ISBN 9781350015555
(paperback) | ISBN 9781350015548 (hardback) | ISBN 9781350015531 (ebook) |
ISBN 9781350015562 (epub)
Subjects: LCSH: Methodology. | Philosophy.
Classification: LCC BD241 .B795 2021 (print) | LCC BD241 (ebook) | DDC 117–dc23
LC record available at https://lccn.loc.gov/2020019590
LC ebook record available at https://lccn.loc.gov/2020019591

ISBN: HB: 978-1-3500-1554-8
PB: 978-1-3500-1555-5
ePDF: 978-1-3500-1553-1
eBook: 978-1-3500-1556-2

Typeset by Deanta Global Publishing Services, Chennai, India
Printed and bound in Great Britain

To find out more about our authors and books visit www.bloomsbury.com and sign up for
our newsletters.

Para Marcelo Svirsky, mi amigo, mi hermano, mi camarada.

Contents

Acknowledgements

I acknowledge support received from the Australian Research Council.

I must thank David Savat, Greg Thompson, Ciara Cremin, Janae Sholtz, Cate Montes, Glen Fuller, Chantelle Gray van Heerden, Joseph Schaal and Stephanie Springgay for wading through countless drafts of this book which seemed not to want to be written.

Thanks and apologies too must also go to my long-suffering editor at Bloomsbury, Liza Thompson!

I would like to thank my many friends in the Latin American Deleuze and Guattari network who through their hospitality, generosity of spirit and intellect helped me to see Deleuze and Guattari through new eyes. In particular, I would like to thank Paúl Palacios, Yolanda Vega and Alberto Leon in Quito; Alfonso Lans and Alfredo Perdomo in Montevideo; Patricio Landaeta in Valparaíso; Axel Cherniavsky and Julian Ferreyra in Buenos Aires; Cristina Póstleman in San Juan; Antonio Amorin and Marcus Novaes in Campinas; Gustavo Chirolla in Bogotá and José Ezcurdia in Mexico City.

I would also like to thank my many friends in the Asian Deleuze and Guattari network who through their hospitality, generosity of spirit and intellect helped me to see Deleuze and Guattari through new eyes. In particular, I would like to thank George Varghese, Saswat Das, Anindya Purakayastha and Manoj Ny in India; Take-Gwang

Lee, Woosung Kang and Jae-Yin Kim in South Korea; Joff Bradley, Koichiro Kokubun and Tatsuya Higaki in Japan; Emily Tsai, Catherine Cheng and Laurie Tseng in Taiwan and Tony See in Singapore.

I would also like to thank my friends in the South African Deleuze and Guattari network who through their hospitality, generosity of spirit and intellect helped me to see Deleuze and Guattari through new eyes. In particular, I would like to thank Chantelle Gray van Heerden, Aragorn Eloff, Andrea Hurst and Bert Olivier.

Special mention must be made too of the heroic work undertaken by Paulo de Assis and Paolo Giudici at the Orpheus Institute in Ghent – the three councils of Ghent (the Deleuze and Artistic Research conferences) have all been wonderful events that I know I have benefited from greatly. Not unrelatedly, I'd like to thank all the convenors of the many Deleuze and Guattari Studies conferences and summer camps that have been held over the past decade or so. Being part of that community is a genuine privilege and a constant source of reassurance that what we do in our university work still matters.

I would also like to thank my current and former PhD students Ryan Frazer, Susie Clements, Dipali Mathur, Peter Goderie and Nikolajs Ozoliņš.

I would also like to thank my fellow adjuncts at the Bellambi Campus of Havana University: Evan Te Ahu Poata-Smith, David Kampers, Andy Davis and our Vice Chancellor Marcelo Svirsky, to whom I dedicate this book in gratitude for more than a decade of friendship. So necessary is he to my intellectual formation that if he did not exist I would have to invent him.

Special thanks must go to Gordon Waitt who has kept me sane in an insane world by constantly reminding me of the value of academic work and thereby giving me reasons to believe in this (academic) world. Our collaborations have enriched me intellectually and spiritually in more ways than I can count or calculate.

Lastly, I must thank my family who have suffered through the writing of this book almost as keenly as I have. To my wife Tanya, I will now make use of that SUP you so kindly gave me as a birthday present; to my children Courtney and Sebastian, I will now go to your sporting events more often and look up from my book more frequently ... and to Chewie, I'll take you for walks more often.

Introduction

Interest in the concept of the assemblage, and by implication the work of Deleuze and Guattari, can be understood, I believe, as a critical response to the growing awareness at the turn of the last century of a new type of social and cultural problem which John Law aptly named 'messy'.[1] 'No doubt some things in the world can indeed be made clear and definite. Income distributions, global CO_2 emissions, the boundaries of nation states, and terms of trade, these are the kinds of provisionally stable realities that social and natural science deal with more or less effectively. But alongside such phenomena the world is also textured in quite different ways.'[2] Unhelpfully, Law tends to collapse all 'non-definite' problems into one 'order' of problem – namely the messy. He avers that '[p]ains and pleasures, hopes and horrors, intuitions and apprehensions, losses and redemptions, mundanities and visions, angels and demons, things that slip and slide, or appear and disappear, change shape or don't have much form at all, unpredictabilities' all fall outside of the range of what social science has traditionally been able to 'capture'.[3] He may well be right in saying this, but it doesn't follow that all these examples can (much less should) be thought in the same way, using the same conceptual framework. If, as Deleuze says, we have the philosophy we deserve according to how well we formulate our problems, then it is important that we take the time to think in a clear and definite way about things that are not themselves clear and definite. In that respect I do not see much advantage in terms like Morton's concept of 'mesh' or Ingold's 'assembly', both of which seem to me to push thinking towards the indefinite and undecided as the best we can hope for, thus making the end point of thinking identical to the starting point, which amounts to a defeat of thought. As Deleuze and Guattari say, 'If one concept is "better" than an earlier one, it is because it makes us aware of new variations and unknown resonances, it carries out unforeseen cuttings-out, it brings forth an Event that surveys us.'[4] Our question should thus be: What does the concept of the assemblage enable us to see that we couldn't see before?

The answer to this question, which many commentators have put to themselves, is surprisingly uniform across the spectrum of responses. In large part, though, this is because so-called assemblage theory, rather than going to the original source, seems content to rely on a handful of commentaries on Deleuze and Guattari for their definition of the concept. Doubtless this is because the original source is complicated, to say the least, and far from easy to strip-mine for straightforward definitions. For example, DeLanda claims that Deleuze and Guattari give assemblage 'half a dozen different interpretations', which he professes to bring together in order to create a unified version of the concept. The trouble is, to do that he modifies the concept, introducing new ways of thinking about the assemblage which, on the one hand, he dismisses as 'harmless' additions and, on the other hand, extols as necessary changes to make the concept immune to certain logical difficulties that are, in DeLanda's view, inherent in Deleuze and Guattari's version of the concept.[5] Simplifying Deleuze and Guattari's thought, as DeLanda tries to do, does not seem to me to be the right way of going about this because, apart from the strange model of scholarship it entails, of avoiding rather than working through conceptual difficulty, it necessarily leads to a diminished understanding of the concept. And yet that tends to be the way most commentators go about dealing with the concept of the assemblage, which no doubt explains both the uniformity of interpretations and the apparent reluctance in the field to return to the original source material. Assemblage has all but become a 'received idea' (as Flaubert put it), that is, an idea that is so well understood it no longer bears thinking about in a critical way.

Accordingly, any *and* every 'thing', or more precisely, any and every kind of *collection of things* has in recent times been called an assemblage. And even more problematically the coming together of every kind of *collection of things* is now referred to as assembling, even though assemblage in Deleuze and Guattari's sense and assembling are not linguistically related and in fact derive from two different words. This constant and seemingly limitless expansion of the term's range of applications begs the question, ever more insistently it seems to me, if any and every kind of collection of things is an assemblage, then what advantage is there in using this term and not some other term, or indeed no term at all? What makes an assemblage an assemblage and not some other kind of collection of things? If any apparently random 'heap of fragments', to use Jameson's suggestive phrase for the 'randomly heterogeneous and fragmentary and the aleatory', is an assemblage then the concept serves only to say either that everything is more organized than it appears, or, on the contrary, that everything is ultimately less organized than it appears. Either the heap of fragments has a secret order we don't see or the apparently ordered totality is really a heap of fragments if only we knew how to look properly.[6] Either way, it does not move us much beyond a highly ambivalent baseline assumption, and we surely have a right to expect more from a new concept. At stake here, I would argue, is the need to distinguish the adjectival from the analytical and to recognize that it is only the latter form that is properly philosophical. Our task here, then, is to isolate and define the specifically Deleuze and Guattarian species of assemblage and evaluate it against other varieties on offer. More often than not this will entail an examination of the hybrids on offer and asking what is gained and what is lost in the changes enacted. For these reasons, and more that I will elaborate throughout this book, I argue that we need to *return to the work of Deleuze and Guattari* if we are to make full use of the concept of the assemblage.[7]

Although at its core assemblage theory clearly arose out of the work of Deleuze and Guattari, particularly *A Thousand Plateaus*, it does not always adhere to their conception of it; indeed, as I argue here, it frequently departs from their work in quite significant ways. Both Actor-Network Theory (ANT), which arose out of the work of Bruno Latour, and New Materialism, which arose out of the work of Manuel DeLanda, Jane Bennett and William Connolly (among others), are prime examples of bodies of work that fit the category of assemblage theory and acknowledge a debt to the work of Deleuze and Guattari but nonetheless go about things in their own way, often in ways that are at odds with the inspirational source. DeLanda admits as much when he offers the conceit that his work might be thought of as a kind of Deleuze 2.0. The difficulties don't stop there because there is also a considerable body of work that falls under the heading of assemblage theory that not only owes nothing at all to the work of Deleuze and Guattari but doesn't even bear a 'family resemblance' to their thinking as both ANT and New Materialism do. So while there can be no question that the concept of the assemblage has generated interesting new ways of thinking about the complex nature of social reality, in the evolutionary leap it made from being a concept confined to the work of Deleuze and Guattari to a global theory it has also drifted a long way from its origins and in doing so a number of both small and large misprisions of Deleuze and Guattari's work have slipped under the radar and embedded themselves as 'truths'.[8] These misprisions are, in some instances, of the order of Harold Bloom's notion of the strong misreading, they are the necessary condition of a certain kind of creative appropriation of Deleuze and Guattari's work, as one might claim is true of both Bruno Latour's and Manuel DeLanda's work, but as I will argue these versions of the assemblage are considerably narrower in scope than the version one finds in Deleuze and Guattari.

One may well answer this judgement by saying that Deleuze and Guattari do not themselves call for strict adherence to their ideas and this is certainly true. But Deleuze also said that his own appropriations of other philosophers, which he freely admitted were monstrous, were always true to their original authors. It was important to him that he didn't put words in their mouth, and that the child he made with them was unmistakably their offspring.[9] It is my contention here that most of the existing appropriations of Deleuze and Guattari's work do not meet this standard and that this matters because the versions of assemblage theory they have given us are in several key ways inferior to the original, to the point where one is in fact forced to call into question their parentage. The first and most important casualty has been the connection to the concept of desire. All references to and considerations of desire are consciously excluded from discussion as either unnecessary or simply too messy. Assemblages are thereby reduced to mere apparatuses, which is precisely not what Deleuze and Guattari intended (they constantly caution us against taking a mechanistic view of things). The second casualty has been the multidimensional nature of the concept of the assemblage. This manifests itself in two ways: on the one hand, the assemblage is treated as a stand-alone concept, which it isn't, and on the other hand, the assemblage is treated as though it consists of only one kind of component, namely the machinic, which is similarly wrong-headed. As a consequence, much of what goes by the name of assemblage theory today is an emaciated and innervated version of the full body of ideas and concepts Deleuze and Guattari bequeathed us. My aim in what follows is to restore to some of that lost conceptual vitality.

In this book, then, I do three things. I return to Deleuze and Guattari's concept of the assemblage. I distinguish their version of the assemblage from other versions that have emerged in the wake of their work. And I try to show how one might go about using their concept of the assemblage for practical applications in social and cultural research. If I spend time pointing out in a detailed way the shortcomings of several key iterations of assemblage theory, it is because they have become (in Deleuze and Guattari's own terms) the *image of the assemblage* and as a consequence they not only get in the way of a clear understanding of the original work, they also impede the necessary labour of experimenting with their ideas to see where they might take us by presenting us with a false picture of an already worked-out theory. Deleuze and Guattari themselves treat the assemblage as a provisional concept for which much 'working out' remained to be done. Unfortunately, neither lived long enough to complete the task, but I would argue that it is an unfinishable task because history itself is unfinished. In the years that followed the publication of *A Thousand Plateaus*, Deleuze quite deliberately returned to his own projects – to find himself again, he said – but Guattari continued to work on and develop the concept of the assemblage, giving us a far richer picture of the concept than can be found in their collaborative work alone (a fact that makes the refusal of erstwhile assemblage theorists like DeLanda to even read Guattari utterly mystifying).

I treat assemblage theory as an *incomplete project* that invites us to develop it further on the basis of a set of 'first principles'. The latter are developed throughout Deleuze and Guattari's work, but there is a coded summary of them in 'The Geology of Morals' chapter in *A*

Thousand Plateaus, which as it is obviously intended as a route map for the entire schizoanalytic project (of which assemblage theory is an essential component) makes a convenient starting place. If any single chapter deserves to be described as playful and poetic, it is this one – as such I offer a detailed reading of it in Chapter 1. 'The Geology of Morals' is far from easy to follow, not least because it is so playful and poetic, but if one reads it carefully it yields a small set of foundational propositions that one can use as a point of entry for the voyage into schizoanalysis (to borrow Virginia Woolf's happy image for the process of reading a long-form text). Like Poe's purloined letter, these propositions are hidden in plain sight and for that reason they can be very difficult to see. Not only that, one always has the feeling that someone – perhaps everyone – is seeing what you cannot, which can be discouraging and not a little bruising. However, we cannot all be like the perspicacious Monsieur Dupin and instantly see through every ruse, so we have to develop ways of stepping back and finding the right perspective to obtain a clear view. Ultimately, we simply need to trust in their advice that we will 'be in a position to understand it later on'[10] and resist the urge to seek what Jameson has appropriately called 'the mischief of premature clarification'.[11]

In the dialogue between Deleuze and Foucault 'Intellectuals and Power', Deleuze says a 'theory is exactly like a box of tools. ... It must be useful. It must function.'[12] He goes onto say that like a new pair of glasses, an image he attributes to Proust, it should be used to see something outside and beyond its point of origin in a specific work. To read Proust is to see the whole of France's Second Empire laid out on the dissecting table; similarly, to read Deleuze and Guattari is to see the whole of late capitalism laid out on the dissecting table. Doubtless this accounts for the notorious complexity of their work; its intellectual ambitions are literally boundless. Nothing less than a complete history of the present of desire is offered in the two volumes of *Capitalism and Schizophrenia*. However, as I will show, in spite of its vast scope, one does not need to dumb down or modify Deleuze and Guattari's thinking in order to find in it a set of tools one can turn to one's own projects. The working parts of their methodology – the tools – are all hidden in plain view. To grasp them one has but to set aside one's presumptions as to what an assemblage should look like.

As Deleuze writes in *Difference and Repetition*, the problem of where to begin in philosophy has always been 'regarded as a very delicate problem, for beginning means eliminating all presuppositions'.[13] In philosophy presuppositions come in two forms, objective and subjective, and it is all too easy to refuse the former only to fall back on the latter without even knowing it. Deleuze gives the example of Descartes who, because he did not want to define humans as rational animals which presupposes the concepts of rationality and animality (in an objective sense), instead proposed the model of the cogito in terms of a thinking subject. In doing so he claimed to have escaped the pitfall of objective presupposition; but it is clear, Deleuze says, that he has not escaped the subterranean danger of subjective presupposition because his definition of the cogito assumes 'that everybody knows, independently of concepts, what is meant by self, thinking, and being.'[14] Descartes's 'I think' only appears to be a philosophical beginning because it has buried its presuppositions in the empirical realm of the self. In this way it fails to question what it necessarily presupposes. He taxes Hegel and Heidegger for making a similar style of error. How, then, are we to avoid making the same mistake? We must, he says, find the modesty to *not* know 'what everybody knows' and to *not* recognize 'what everybody is supposed to recognize.'[15] Only then can we be without presuppositions. My task in this book is to try to bring to bear this way of thinking to the notion of the assemblage, which has become one of those concepts like différance, ideology and performativity that everybody knows and everybody recognizes.

Inevitably, it seems, this brings us to the question that no one, not even the authors themselves, can avoid, namely how should we read Deleuze and Guattari? Their work is as playful and poetic as it is vast in scope and ambition. There are of course varying opinions as to the best way to proceed, but undoubtedly it is Brian Massumi's advice that one should approach *A Thousand Plateaus* as one does a record (a now outdated technological reference – the contemporary equivalent I suppose is a YouTube or Spotify playlist), which allows that one may skip sections, that has had the most traction. This advice no doubt comes as a relief to anyone struggling to make sense of a particular section, because it excuses the urge to jump ahead and skim over the parts that don't make immediate sense. Hence its popularity. The problem with Massumi's advice, though, is that it assumes either that one can come to grips with the central arguments of Deleuze and Guattari's work in an ad hoc fashion or that there is in fact no central argument that one needs to come to grips with and the work itself is ad hoc. While it is true that there is a high level of redundancy across the chapters such that if one misses something in one place one may pick it up elsewhere, there is also synthesis which demands that it be read in sequence. As Deleuze explains, the chapters of *A Thousand Plateaus* are 'like a set of split rings. You can fit any one of them into any other.'[16] The trap for the unwary, however, is the way the concepts evolve and even change name and appearance as the book unfolds. If one misses this, then one risks treating concepts like the body without organs and the plane of immanence as distinct, when in actuality they are two faces of the same concept, which has several other faces as well.

If one were to use a musical analogy here for the way *A Thousand Plateaus* is composed it would be the notion of theme and variation, whereby a musical motif is introduced and steadily varied throughout the composition until it becomes all but unrecognizable (the third movement of Beethoven's ninth symphony is one of the more well-known examples of this technique). Variation is an essential idea underpinning the entire schizoanalytic project, so this analogy is doubly appropriate. Variation can only be appreciated fully if one has a sense of the whole piece, which one simply cannot get by skipping sections or listening to it out of sequence. It is true that Deleuze and Guattari do say *A Thousand Plateaus* can be read in any order, but they also say the conclusion can only be read at the end, that is, when one has a solid grasp of the whole project. In other words, it doesn't matter how you get to an understanding of the whole just so long as you do. My sense though is that it is bad advice, reading it out sequence compounds the possibilities of misunderstanding by creating the false impression that the work isn't underpinned by a coherent logic, or building towards a composite understanding of the world. It is also true that Deleuze says that it is good to read a book as one listens to a record, but I would argue his purpose is to put the book on the same level as music, film and the cultural arts in general, not to suggest as Massumi implies that one should allow one's taste to dictate one's progress through the work.

This problem of how to approach *A Thousand Plateaus*, which Massumi rightly broaches, is raised to an even greater order of difficulty when one asks, where in fact does *A Thousand Plateaus* begin and end? Does it begin with *Anti-Oedipus*? Or does one need to go further back, and if so how far back? Does it include everything Deleuze wrote prior to meeting Guattari? Does it end with *What is Philosophy*? Does it also include everything Deleuze and Guattari wrote separately after *A Thousand Plateaus* was published? Should one read all their source materials as well? I have always thought that Deleuze and Guattari only ever had one project – the invention of schizoanalysis – and that it began before they met and it continued after they stopped explicitly working together and it didn't stop with their deaths. It continued both because it couldn't be brought to completion by them (because there was always something new for them to consider) and because the conditions that prompted its invention, namely late capitalism, continue to obtain. Deleuze was already working on a version of schizoanalysis even before he met Guattari, just as Guattari was already working on a version of schizoanalysis before he met Deleuze. That is how and why they met. Deleuze wanted to talk to someone who worked with schizophrenics in order to test certain ideas he was developing about the language of schizophrenia and his former student suggested he get in touch with Guattari. Meanwhile Guattari had been working on some ideas about the machinic way schizophrenia worked using Deleuze's book *The Logic of Sense*, so when he was offered the chance to meet Deleuze he didn't hesitate.

Their relationship has been caricatured by people who should know better (i.e. Alain Badiou and Slavoj Žižek) as one in which the 'pure' philosopher Deleuze was politicized by the 'activist' Guattari. But aside from the underlying bad faith of such judgements, this caricature fails to pay attention to what they themselves say about their collaboration. In *Dialogues*, the book Deleuze wrote with Claire Parnet in between *Anti-Oedipus* and *A Thousand Plateaus* (this is how Deleuze himself puts it[17]), Deleuze tells a beautiful story about the way he worked with Guattari that makes it clear that it wasn't a simple case of one radicalizing the other. Deleuze has his own word for it, he calls it a pick-up procedure (he rejects the word 'method'). 'Félix was working on black holes; this astronomical idea fascinated him. The black hole is what captures you and does not let you get out. ... I was working, rather, on a white wall: what is a white wall, a screen, how do you plane down the wall and make a line of flight pass? We had not brought the two ideas together, but we noticed that each was tending of its own accord towards the other, to produce something which, indeed, was neither in the one nor the other. For black holes on a white wall are in fact a face. … Now it no longer resembles a face, it is rather the assemblage or the abstract machine which produces the face. Suddenly the problem bounces back and it is political: which societies and civilizations need this machine to function?'[18] Every one of their concepts can be traced back to this singular question, which is not 'how does it work?' but 'why is it happening?' In order to answer this question they draw on the resources of every available intellectual system, which is what Deleuze means by pick-up method. It implies a convergence and collaboration between all forms of scholarly endeavour. In many ways it is this aspect of their work that has been the most influential, especially with scholars who do not read their work.

Although it draws on a disconcertingly heterogeneous range of material – here it helps to remember that they enlisted the aid of their students to compile this material over the course of seven years of teaching together – it is nonetheless a highly coherent body of work. And it is precisely the assemblage understood as a multidimensional concept that holds it all together. That the concept of the assemblage is the engine that drives Deleuze and Guattari's entire critical project is signalled by Deleuze himself in three brief remarks made in the course of an interview with Catherine Clément following the publication of *A Thousand Plateaus*. Asked point-blank what holds *A Thousand Plateaus* together, Deleuze replies, 'I think it is the idea of an assemblage (which replaces the idea of desiring machines).'[19] As Deleuze explains in the discussion following his 1973 conference presentation published in English as 'Five Propositions on Psychoanalysis,' he and Guattari felt compelled to jettison the term 'desiring-machine' because they felt trapped by it – too many people were using it, co-opting it and thereby domesticating it (one can only imagine how they'd feel about the word assemblage if they were alive today). Only a year after the publication of *Anti-Oedipus* Deleuze and Guattari were already concerned that 'desiring-machine' had lost its capacity to upset people.[20] But they were also moving on conceptually and in this sense the concept of the assemblage is not merely a new word for an old concept, it is a point of departure – it answers to a new problematic. As Deleuze explains in an interview published in *Libération* upon the publication of *A Thousand Plateaus*, the aim of the new book is to interrogate 'the circumstances in which things happen: in what situations, where and when does a particular thing happen, how does it happen, and so on?'[21] The assemblage is intended to answer several types of question, 'how?', 'why?', 'when?' and not just a 'what?' question.[22]

This leads me to the second remark I want to underscore because it goes to the heart of the entire schizoanalytic project. Deleuze tells Clément that he and Guattari 'are trying to substitute the idea of the assemblage for the idea of behaviour: whence the importance of ethology, and the analysis of animal assemblages, e.g. territorial assemblages'.[23] To which he adds an important and frequently overlooked clarification: the assemblage is first of all a problem of consistency and this is 'prior to the problem of behaviour'.[24] Ethology is a means of formulating a problem – the problem of desire – not the answer to the problem, nor the means to answering the problem. The same must be said for all of the scientific research Deleuze and Guattari draw on – they use it to formulate problems and create concepts, not as reference material.[25] While it is obvious Deleuze and Guattari drew a great deal of inspiration from the work of Uexküll, Tinbergen, Lorenz and others, it is equally clear that their work departs quite fundamentally from it as well. If we must connect it to ethology, then I think we need to see it as a reinvention of ethology rather than an extension of it, one that instigates a radical shift of ground away from an idea of nature dominated by the involuntary promptings of our base instincts (however conceived). If we don't, then the risk is that we will reduce the assemblage to a biological system, or worse a set of instincts, that governs behaviour in a determinate manner, when precisely the opposite of that is what is at stake. To put it another way, it would not be much of a victory if we broke free of the iron grip of Freud's Oedipal models only to wind up in the similarly restrictive arms of Uexküll, for as interesting and as insightful as the latter is, his work offers only the most marginal of insights into the complexities of human behaviour in the twentieth and twenty-first centuries. And as is clear from the quotation at the head of this chapter, Deleuze and Guattari ultimately thought the notion of behaviour as it was formulated by ethology was flawed.[26]

The third remark I want to focus on occurs a few lines after those cited above. Deleuze tells Clément that he and Guattari have themselves only begun to develop what he refers to as the 'general logic' of assemblages, and he expects that completing it will occupy them in the future. Sadly this was not to be, at least not in their work together. *What is Philosophy?* moves away from the central themes of *Anti-Oedipus* and *A Thousand Plateaus* and takes an inward turn to look at the constitution of philosophy itself. From the perspective of assemblage theory it adds very little except the important reminder that chaos is the essential ground zero of desire for both Deleuze and Guattari – it is what desire in its free state looks like, it is the source of all creativity and at the same time it threatens all forms with dissolution. Deleuze's own books, written in between *A Thousand Plateaus* and *What is Philosophy?*, similarly add little to the assemblage theory project. As I have argued elsewhere, Deleuze's two books on cinema are something of a missed opportunity in this respect because the one question they consistently avoid asking is precisely the schizoanalytic question of why would anyone want to watch this or that film?[27] By contrast, Guattari's work in the years after *A Thousand Plateaus* is almost exclusively devoted to the development and expansion of the 'general logic' of assemblages. There are two points here that I want to underscore. First, Deleuze and Guattari conceived of assemblages as having a 'general logic'. This means we cannot start from single assemblages and work our way up – we have to start 'all at once' as one does with language (which is not to say assemblages are structured like a language). Second, the fact that Deleuze and Guattari saw that their project was incomplete means not only that we have an opportunity to complete it ourselves, but also that we need to be vigilant against premature attempts to bring the process to a close, which would only be possible if history itself had come to a standstill.

Asked if it wasn't a paradox for a work like *A Thousand Plateaus* to consider itself a system, Deleuze said while it had become commonplace to say knowledge systems have broken down and that knowledge is so fragmented that it was no longer possible to construct systems, it was completely false to think that systems thinking had lost its power. 'There are two problems with this idea: people can't imagine doing any serious work except on very restricted and specific little series; worse still, any broader approach is left to the spurious work of visionaries, with anyone saying whatever comes into their head.' Despite the various critiques of poststructuralism, postmodernism and deconstruction, systems have not lost their philosophical power according to Deleuze, because they have been rethought as open rather than closed systems. 'What I and Guattari call a rhizome' he says 'is precisely an open system.'[28] Deleuze and Guattari were not, as many people seem to think, opposed to the idea of something being expressible as a whole.[29] Indeed, the reality is without it neither the abstract machine nor the body without organs nor the assemblage would be thinkable as concepts. Deleuze and Guattari conceive of the concept of the whole, borrowing from Proust, as 'a product, produced as nothing more than a part alongside other parts, which it neither unifies nor totalizes, though it has an effect on these other parts because it establishes paths of communication between noncommunicating vessels, transverse unities between unities between elements that retain all their differences within their own particular boundaries.'[30] As they go onto say, the whole is poorly understood if it is treated as either the sum of its parts or an original totality; rather, as with Proust's novel, it comes into being as the synthetic product of the work and at the same time sits above the work (superlinearity), simultaneously surveying every corner of its created universe and policing its boundaries.

This is perhaps the moment for me to say that my version of the assemblage owes nothing to the work of Manuel DeLanda, except perhaps as a useful reminder of why it is important to read Deleuze and Guattari carefully. DeLanda treats the assemblage as an aggregate, albeit a complex aggregate of the variety of an ecosystem. Nonetheless, for DeLanda the assemblage is an entity that grows in both scale and complexity as components are added. In his view, assemblages are 'wholes whose properties emerge from the interactions between parts'. He suggests they can be used to 'model' 'entities' such 'interpersonal networks', 'social justice movements', 'cities' and 'nation-states'.[31] Central to DeLanda's thinking about assemblages is Deleuze's idea (drawn from Hume) that relations are exterior to their terms. This enables DeLanda to offer an account of assemblages as ontologically 'unique, singular, historically contingent, [and] individual'.[32] More particularly, though, DeLanda frames the assemblage as a new way of thinking about part-whole relations, essentially pitching it as a new kind of causality, that is, one that acts without conscious intention or purpose.

For example, during the seventeenth and eighteenth centuries in Europe the authority structure of many organisations changed from a form based on traditional legitimacy to one based on rational-legal bureaucratic procedures. The change affected not only government bureaucracies, but also hospitals, school and prisons. When studied in detail, however, no deliberate plan can be discerned, the change occurring through the slow replacement over two centuries of one set of daily routines by another. Although this replacement did involve decisions by individual persons ... the details of these decisions are in most cases causally redundant to explain the outcome.[33]

There are a number of problems here, but I will focus on just three 'fatal flaws' in DeLanda's account: first, the assemblage does not constitute a part-whole relation; second, the assemblage is not the product of an accumulation of individual acts; and third, the assemblage does not change incrementally. To say that a bureaucratic structure of authority was constituted by and ultimately transformed by myriad individual acts says nothing but the obvious. One does not even need a concept to make this claim. This is history in the mode of one damn thing after another (as Arnold Toynbee famously put it). I will elaborate this briefly by turning to Deleuze and Guattari's account of the formation of the state in *Anti-Oedipus*. As will be immediately obvious, it follows a path that is diametrically opposite to the one mapped out by DeLanda. 'The State was not formed in progressive stages; it appears fully armed, a master stroke executed all at once; the primordial *Urstaat*, the eternal model of everything the State wants to be and desires.'[34] History is *in* the *Urstaat*, in its head, not the other way round: primitive society knew about the terrors of the state, Deleuze and Guattari argue (following Pierre Clastres), long before any actual states existed. Their rituals and customs, centred on the destruction of accumulated 'wealth' (i.e. stockpiles of seeds, weapons, furs and so on) so as to institute a socially binding debt-relation within the 'tribe' and between 'tribes', can be seen as staving off the formation of an actual state, which requires accumulated wealth (i.e. capital) to come into being. It is the idea of the state that concerns Deleuze and Guattari, not the practical matter of its coming into being.[35]

DeLanda thus departs from Deleuze and Guattari in three crucial ways: first, he always proceeds from the concrete to the abstract, whereas Deleuze and Guattari (following Marx's famous reversal of Hegel) tend to proceed from the abstract to the concrete – the state is first of all an idea, it only subsequently functions as a structure of authority; second, it seems he cannot countenance a purely immanent form of organization that isn't somehow undergirded by the transcendent 'real', whereas Deleuze and Guattari say the exact opposite – the state can only function as it does to the extent that it can become immanent; and, third, he reverses the actual-virtual relation – he assumes that the concrete 'bits and pieces' are the actual – whereas for Deleuze and Guattari it is the structure of authority that is actual and the 'bits and pieces' that are virtual.[36] Marcus and Saka, indirectly following DeLanda, thus write that the assemblage 'is a topological concept that designates the actualizations of the virtual causes or causal processes that are immanent in an open system of intensities that is under the influence of a force that is external (or heterogeneous) in relation to it'.[37] But this is precisely the wrong way round: *only the actual elements can be causal*. It is very clear in their discussion of the 'actual factor' in desiring-production that the actual is what is self-generated and therefore active in the unconscious, while the virtual is the imported and therefore inert or 'dead' element in the unconscious (e.g. they describe the Oedipal complex as virtual).[38]

Lastly, I need to say something about the word 'assemblage' itself because there is a tendency apparent in much of 'assemblage theory' today to treat the word 'assemblage' in what might be called a 'plain language' fashion, as though the meaning of the concept is self-evident from the choice of word. This can be seen in its application in the social sciences, where there is an emerging emphasis on the process of assembling itself.[39] This way of approaching the concept is only possible if one forgets or overlooks the fact that 'assemblage' is a translation of 'agencement'. Perhaps because of its Francophone appearance – it is in fact a 'loan' word adopted from the French – it is assumed that it is the same word Deleuze and Guattari used and in the manner say of Derrida's concept of 'différance' it has been left untranslated. At conferences one often hears presenters pronouncing 'assemblage' in an exaggeratedly French manner, suggesting that they think it is a French word, rather than a translation of a French word. By these subtle turns then the false idea that 'assemblage' is the original word and therefore the word one needs to explore in order to appreciate fully the concept's range of meanings has become thoroughly entrenched as a 'received idea'. Adding to the confusion, Deleuze and Guattari do occasionally use the French word 'assemblage' as well, but as John Phillips points out, never in the same technical or philosophical sense that they give to 'agencement'.[40]

Assemblage is Paul Patton and Paul Foss's choice of translation for *agencement* which Brian Massumi picked up and used in his translation of *A Thousand Plateaus*. It has since become more or less the default translation, despite the fact that – as several people have pointed out[41] – it has its problems.[42] In my view, however, these problems are not resolved by altering the translation and using a different word, but rather by problematizing it and opening it up to a more complicated reading, one that is more consciously attentive to Deleuze and Guattari's work. I would add that I think there is probably a strong case to be made for leaving it untranslated, as is increasingly the case with translations of critical theory concepts today, though that itself carries the risk of hypostatizing the term in a different way. Agencement derives from *agencer*, which according to *Le Roberts*

Collins means 'to arrange, to lay out, or to piece together', whereas assemblage means 'to join, to gather, to assemble'.[43] Agencement, as John Law has noted, encompasses a range of meanings that include 'to arrange, to dispose, to fit up, to combine, to order'.[44] It could therefore just as appropriately be translated as arrangement, in the sense of a 'working arrangement', provided it was kept clear that it described an ongoing process rather than a static situation.[45] It could also be thought in terms of a 'musical arrangement', which is a way of adapting an abstract plan of music to a particular performer and performance. Arrangement is in many ways my preferred translation for these reasons, but it also has its problems, not least the fact it obscures the fact that 'agency' is at its core. So I wouldn't say I disagree with Patton's original choice, which like all translations has its problems but is very far from being wrong or inappropriate and I certainly think it is considerably better than several other choices that have also been tried.[46] But it is equally clear that it is a word that needs to be used with caution if we are not to fall into the trap of what I have called a plain-language conception of it.

Very quickly, then, I want to make two observations about the way Deleuze and Guattari use the word 'agencement' that foreshadows the trajectory I will follow in this book. To begin with, it is useful to note that *agencement* is Deleuze and Guattari's own translation, or perhaps rearrangement would be a better word, of the German word *Komplex* (as in the 'Oedipal complex' or the 'castration complex'). Although it is Guattari himself who defines the assemblage in this way in the various glossaries he has provided, the connection between Freud's notion of complex and the concept of the assemblage has been almost completely ignored. If there is any word whose meaning one should explore as a way into assemblage theory then it is complex. According to Laplanche and Pontalis's exhaustive account, there are three senses of the word complex in Freud's writing: (1) 'a relatively stable arrangement of chains of association'; (2) 'a collection of personal characteristics – including the best integrated ones – which is organised to a greater or lesser degree, the emphasis here being on emotional reactions'; (3) 'a basic structure of interpersonal relationships and the way in which the individual finds and appropriates his place'.[47] Laplanche and Pontalis also note that there is an underlying tendency towards 'psychologism' inherent in the term. Not only does it imply that all individual behaviour is shaped by a latent, unchanging structure, it also allows that there is a complex for every conceivable psychological type. The key point I want to make here is that none of these ways of thinking about the complex actually requires that we give any consideration to a material object.

The second observation I want to offer is to note that in his comments on Man Ray's piece 'dancer/danger', Guattari (in his essay 'Balancing-Sheet Program for Desiring Machines', which was appended to the second edition of *Anti-Oedipus* and can therefore be read as a kind of bridging piece linking *Anti-Oedipus* to *A Thousand Plateaus*) observes that what is crucial about this assemblage is the fact that it doesn't work. He means this quite literally. The working parts, its cogs and wheels and so on, do not turn or intermesh with one another in a mechanical fashion. It is precisely for that reason, he argues, that it *works* as a piece of art.[48] It works by creating an association (i.e. a refrain) between the human dancer and the inhuman machine, and thereby brings them into a new kind of relation which he and Deleuze would later call the assemblage, but in their first works they called the desiring-machine. The only time they make a direct comparison between the unconscious and actual machines is when they compare it to the absurd machines of the Dadaists, surrealists, as well as the infernal machines imagined by Buster Keaton and Rube Goldberg.[49] And again, what is crucial is that these machines don't work. In other words, the obvious mechanical explanation of various machines is precisely *not* what Deleuze and Guattari had in mind when they conceived of the concept of the assemblage and its forerunner, the desiring-machine.

As Deleuze and Guattari say, 'Thinkers who do not renew the image of thought are not philosophers but functionaries who, enjoying a ready-made thought, are not even conscious of the problem and are unaware even of the efforts of those they claim to take as their models.'[50] Concepts should bring about a new way of seeing something and not simply fix a label to something we think we already know about. For Deleuze and Guattari the critical analytic question is always: Given a specific situation what kind of assemblage would be required to produce it?

1

The Problem of Strata

When Charles Darwin decided to accept Captain FitzRoy's invitation to join the HMS *Beagle's* voyage to South America he was equally excited about the prospect of exploring new and strange geological formations as he was of finding new and strange species of plants and animals. And though he tends to be remembered for his writing about animals, particularly his theory of how they evolved, it should not be forgotten that he also wrote extensively on geology because it was his interest in the nature of the earth's crust that drove him to rethink the natural history of the earth's inhabitants. As an earnest young university student, Darwin had the opportunity to entertain one of his professors, the geologist Adam Sedgwick, at his family home in Shrewsbury, prior to their planned fieldwork trip to the North of Wales to explore its geology. Keen to impress his illustrious mentor, Darwin told him the story of a local manual labourer's discovery of a tropical shell found in a nearby gravel pit. Sedgwick laughed at him. 'If the shell was genuinely embedded there, said Sedgwick, it would overthrow everything that was known about the superficial deposits of the Midland counties.'[1] Sedgwick concluded it must have been left there by someone and took no further interest in it. Darwin, however, never stopped thinking about it and never forgot this episode. In later life he would recall being astonished that Sedgwick was not excited by this strange fact, as he was, and disappointed that he was willing to simply dismiss as aberrant anything that didn't agree with his sense of how things are and therefore must be. By contrast, Darwin, who was an avid and early reader of Charles Lyell, who would go on to become one of the most renowned geologists of the Victorian era (unsurprisingly Sedgwick had no time for Lyell), was willing to set aside everything that was thought to be known about geology – including of course all the theologically inflected knowledge about the subject – in order to explain this one curious fact. What is interesting about this moment, for our purposes here, is that the geology of the earth was not well understood in Darwin's time, and it was a long way from attaining the status it has today of scientific knowledge. As such, it was subject to theoretical speculation.

As the late palaeontologist Stephen Jay Gould reminds us, it was ever thus and remains so today. Science advances via speculation, which it then tries to prove (or falsify) via experimentation. Although our technology today is vastly more sophisticated than anything the Victorians could call upon, we remain just as reliant on theoretical speculation to resolve what may appear to be purely material problems today as we did in Darwin's time. 'Reality does not speak to us objectively, and no scientist can be free from constraints of psyche and society. The greatest impediment to scientific innovation is usually a conceptual lock not a factual lack.'[2] Gould's book *Wonderful Life*, a marvellous history of the discovery, interpretation and reinterpretation of the Burgess Shale, the vast trove of fossils which provided the first evidence of the so-called Cambrian explosion, offers an extended demonstration of this point and in doing so reiterates the importance of the problem identified above, namely the problem of presupposition, only on a much grander scale. As Deleuze said, it is a delicate problem, not easily overcome because one is not usually aware of the degree to which one is in the grips of a presupposition.[3] There is perhaps no better illustration of this than the story of the discovery and more especially the first interpretation of the Burgess Shale. The honour of finding the Burgess Shale fossils goes to Charles Doolittle Walcott, then head of the Smithsonian, who stumbled across them in a quarry in British Columbia in the late summer of 1909. His discovery changed the course of modern palaeontology, or at least it would have done if 'Walcott [hadn't] proceeded to misinterpret these fossils in a comprehensive and thoroughly consistent manner arising directly from his conventional view of life. In short, he shoehorned every last Burgess animal into a modern group, viewing the fauna collectively as a set of primitive or ancestral versions of later, improved forms.'[4] Walcott's twofold error (to put it into philosophical terms) was to assume that the present can explain the past and that the past must have a representative today in however changed form.

What Walcott did not allow for (because he couldn't imagine it or conceptualize it, just as Sedgwick could neither imagine nor conceptualize that Shrewsbury had once been under the ocean) was the extinction of phyla. It is now estimated that fifteen or so different phyla are evident in the Burgess Shale, perhaps more, of which only four can claim modern ancestors, but Walcott failed to notice this because he assumed the past must be symmetrical with the present. He assumed that everything he found must have a modern representative, so he overlooked genuine differences in kind, reducing them to mere differences of degree, in order to preserve his key presupposition about the absolute number of phyla.[5] As such, he never realized just how incredible his discovery really was. Because of the esteem in which Walcott was held in his own lifetime, it wasn't until several decades after his death that fresh eyes re-examined his discoveries and began to piece together the radical truth that eluded him. For Gould this story is interesting for a number of reasons, as a cautionary tale about the perils of not challenging one's presuppositions, as a scientific adventure story every bit as thrilling intellectually as an Indiana Jones film (minus the whips and Nazis, of course), but most importantly as supporting evidence of his own hypothesis that evolution was not gradual and progressive as Darwin had supposed but contingent and brutal. 'The history of life is a story of massive removal followed by differentiation within a few surviving stocks, not the conventional tale of steadily increasing excellence, complexity, and diversity.'[6] What strata tell us, according to Gould, is that history is profoundly contingent, a view that Deleuze and Guattari explicitly support. 'A historical explanation does not rest on direct deductions from laws of nature, but on an unpredictable sequence of antecedent states, where any major change in any step of the sequence would have altered the final result.'[7] This, I will argue, is central to how we should begin to think about strata: it maps the relations of dependency that exist between various moments in history that taken together produce the present as we know it.

As Gould argues, though, relations of dependency must also take into account that which has disappeared from history – our present is the sum both of the paths taken and the paths not taken. In short, we should not assume that the assemblages of today are more perfect forms of the assemblages of yesterday. What this detour via Gould helps us to see, which I want to suggest is critical to understanding Deleuze and Guattari's deployment of the concept of strata, is that strata are first of all a way of *problematizing appearances*. Strata are the conceptual means of transforming that which seems to have been given by either god or nature into something that is the product of multiple processes and forces over time. Strata transform nature into history and history into nature. Strata are the product of the manifold processes that have over time constructed and produced the thing we call nature, whether by that we mean human nature or nature as wilderness. We have to be careful not to reverse this historicizing process by overemphasizing the apparent 'naturalness' of strata, that is, by forgetting that 'strata' refers to a concept that enables us to see and think about a certain type of process, the production of nature, not the thing itself. Quite literally, until the Danish scholar Nicolas Steno (Niels Steensen) proposed to think about the layering of rocks he saw in his travels around Italy as strata that had been formed in a particular sequence, no one saw anything but rocks they assumed had been formed all at once in the moment of the earth's creation.[8] His speculation defamiliarized the Tuscan landscape, punctuating its apparent timelessness with the segmentations of science and history. His conclusion, however, was altogether unscientific and ahistorical; in his mind, the existence of geological stratification proved that the world had indeed been inundated with water, just as it says in the Bible.[9] The lesson to be drawn from this, then, is not that we can use stratigraphy to understand contemporary society, as though it somehow resembles geological formations.[10] Rather, the lesson is that in order to begin to analyse contemporary society we need to construe it as a *problematic field*. Just as Darwin wondered how a seashell came to be in a gravel pit in the Midlands, so we need to wonder how it is that our world is populated by similarly inexplicable phenomena from President Trump to K-pop and look for a systematic explanation.

To begin with, though, we need to start by problematizing the notion of stratification itself because it is far from clear how one should define it, much less use it. And yet, as I will argue, it is absolutely pivotal to any possible use of the concept of the assemblage. Stratification has received comparatively little attention in the secondary literature on Deleuze and Guattari. There are two reasons for this neglect, I suspect: for a start it seems kind of obvious what it means, it appears to be basic high school geology after all, so there's no apparent need to inquire too deeply as to what Deleuze and Guattari actually meant by it; and, because it seems kind of obvious what it means there is no apparent reason to interrogate anyone else's deployment of it either. However, judging by the various quite scanty attempts to define it in the secondary literature it isn't very well understood at all. In fact, given how divergent the various accounts of strata are I think we can safely jettison the idea that its meaning is obvious. That most attempts to explain stratification fall back on elementary geography is itself a dead giveaway that the concept has neither been interrogated nor understood because it ignores the simple fact that evolutionary biology and language philosophy are also called upon by Deleuze and Guattari in their construction of the concept of stratification. It also misses the fact that it is acoustics (which to be fair isn't specifically mentioned) that is the most useful point of reference for understanding strata even though three key acoustical concepts are repeated like a refrain throughout: waves, frequency and resonance. Strata are not inert, in other words, as DeLanda and others seem to think, and certainly cannot be thought of as frozen assemblages as he put it.[11]

What is stratification? I want to give several answers to this question because I think it serves a number of different purposes in Deleuze and Guattari's work, not all of which are signposted and not all of which are explicitly intended by the authors. My priority, though, will be to try to give as accurate a technical definition of it as I can based on a detailed reading of Deleuze and Guattari's work. But before I do that I want to try to give a 'big picture' view of it because it is my sense – my personal experience, I should perhaps say – that the more one drills down into the technical details of Deleuze and Guattari's inventions the harder it is to see how they work in the world beyond their pages. We are at constant risk of becoming 'stuck' on a detail like Bergotte and his little patch of yellow in Vermeer, or Vintueil and his ever elusive little phrase. Deleuze and Guattari specify that there are three types of strata – the geological, the biological and the alloplastic or what I will call the techno-semiological (i.e. humans)

– each of which is composed of a different combination of two key variables, content and expression. Importantly, the relation between these two variables is different for each stratum. This has two crucial implications: it means that there is no direct correspondence between the different strata – one stratum cannot be used to explain another – and that each one has different capacities not necessarily shared by the others (which reinforces the necessity of the previous point). The most important function of the strata I would argue is that they problematize and map the terrain of human existence in a very particular way that can perhaps be visualized along the lines of three dimensional chess, providing we modify the rules so that only the pieces on the top level are capable of moving across all the planes. It amounts to saying, 'we' humans depend on the properties of the earth for our existence (geology) and 'we' depend on the properties of our bodies for what 'we' can do on the earth (biology), but 'we' constantly exceed those limits in the outpourings of our minds. This is the *essential* difference between geological and biological strata and the techno-semiological stratum – the production of signs (both symbols and language) enables the third stratum to translate the other two and in a sense range beyond them.[12] The third stratum is 'alloplastic' whereas the first and second are 'homoplastic'.[13]

In other words, contra DeLanda, assemblage theory does not avoid *essentialism*, it entrenches it at its very heart: geology, biology and techno-semiology are formed differently, they evolved differently, and are defined by an organization of relations that is specific to each stratum.[14] The distinction between the two major variables, content and expression, is different on each stratum, which in turn means that the way each stratum develops is also different. The geological stratum proceeds via *induction*, the biological stratum proceeds via *transduction* and the techno-semiological stratum proceeds by *translation*. In each case, what is *essential* is the increased autonomy of expression and hence the capacity for deterritorialization. In the geological stratum, the distinction between content and expression corresponds to the distinction between the molecular (content) and the molar (expression) and can be understood in terms of orders of magnitude.[15] The molar in this instance is an expression of the molecular. But this distribution does not hold as we move onto the biological stratum. Orders of magnitude continue to be important, but now expression is linear and autonomous from content – the sequencing of the DNA is what gives shape to the organic stratum. It is no longer a matter of volume. Now content and expression are found in both the molecular and molar orders.[16] The techno-semiological stratum is different again. Whereas the organic stratum is defined by spatial linearity, the techno-semiological stratum is defined by superlinearity – language, to give only the most privileged example, is not just a matter of a linear sequence of words and phrases, it also entails synthesis because words combine to form meanings, which are ephemeral events rather than composites of materials, and these combinations can be changed at will (breaking the rules of language produces poetry).[17] What interests Deleuze and Guattari, though, is the way these essentially different strata impact on each other without ceasing to be essentially different from each other (see Steno's first rule of strata).

'Maps should be made of these things' Deleuze and Guattari say, 'organic, ecological, and technological maps one can lay out on a plane of consistency.'[18] These maps should identify what I will call (following Hjelmslev) *orders of dependency*. 'The principle of analysis must ... be a recognition of ... dependences. It must be possible to conceive of parts to which the analysis shall lead as nothing but intersection points of bundles of lines of dependence.'[19] That is to say, analysis should proceed by breaking down an object to its smallest components or terminals as Hjelmslev calls them. For Hjelmslev analysis consists in the 'description of an object by the uniform dependences of other objects on it and on each other. The object that is subjected to analysis we shall call a *class*, and the other objects, which are registered by a particular analysis as uniformly dependent on the class and on each other, we shall call *components* of the class.'[20] Hjelmslev goes onto say that the components can be related in one of two ways: either by means of conjunction – for example, by combining the letters 'p', 'e' and 't' to form the word 'pet' – or disjunction – for example, by recognizing that we could substitute a different letter at any point in that chain to form a new word.[21] As such, the mapping of orders of dependency needs to take into account what I will call a *power of selection* to explain why one component is included and not another. We can use these two principles – order of dependency and power of selection – as a rudimentary navigational aid, a bit like a compass made from magnetized pin on a cork, to assist us in making our way through the dark waters of the mostly implicit methodological aspects of assemblage theory. It gives us two very useful questions to ask as a way of beginning our analysis of a specific social and cultural phenomenon: first, what is the class of object we are dealing with and what are its components? – this is a question of scale, that is, where does an object begin and end? – and, second, what type of relation obtains between the components? and what gives the class consistency? – this is a question of hierarchy and selection, that is, which components belong to a particular class and which do not? Both content and expression exhibit these two principles.

Deleuze and Guattari's interrogation of the phalanx is a useful illustration of this point.[22] The phalanx is the class and the soldiers, their long spear, short dagger, metal chest plate, two-handled shield and so on are the components of that class, each piece in its own way dependent upon the other. At first glance the class is produced additively (synthesis of conjunction), that is, soldier plus shield plus spear plus dagger and so on; but, one can also see the choices are anything but accidental – if a soldier is in a phalanx then he needs a spear (synthesis of connection); and, of course each of these choices is made in the face of several other possibilities (synthesis of disjunction). But these elements by themselves will not yield a phalanx because the phalanx is in actuality an *event*, or rather several events ramifying one another. The phalanx should be understood as a performative in other words. In order to hold tight in phalanx formation the soldiers had to forsake mobility, they had to put their life on the line for those who stood behind them and they had to be prepared to step into the breach should the man in front of them fall, and most of all they had to hold their nerve because if they broke formation a rout would likely ensue. But the questions don't end there because one must also inquire as to what kind of society wants or needs not merely a standing army (for purely defensive purposes), but an expeditionary army formed with the intent of attacking and conquering other countries and peoples? This points us to the existence of another class implicated by the first. The first one was the class of content (the phalanx), whereas this is the class of expression (militarism). It has different components, such as courage, honour, valour and discipline and a different hierarchy of values such as the willingness to kill or die for a compatriot and a cause versus self-protection and self-interest, and so on. It is impossible to say which comes first, the phalanx or the conquering intent, and in that sense we are led to the concept of strata as the necessary unity of these two formations – an assemblage of bodies and weapons on the one hand and an assemblage of imperial ambition and militaristic society on the other. But what we can say is that something $= x$ – a unifying force, let's say – is required to bring these two different orders together. We can also say that a something $= x$ – an initiating cause or quasi-cause, let's say – was required to initiate these two orders – neither the phalanx nor the militarist ideology that harnesses it appeared spontaneously.

Stratification is a function in Hjelmslev's terms with two dimensions: content and expression.[23] These same two dimensions are the working parts of Deleuze and Guattari's concept of the assemblage; but they are not the only parts (the body without organs and abstract machine must also be considered components of the concept of the assemblage). Both these dimensions themselves and the relation between them are purely arbitrary. As Hjelmslev puts it, the two dimensions 'are defined only by their mutual solidarity, and neither of them can be identified otherwise. They are defined only oppositively and relatively, as mutually opposed functives of one and the same function.'[24] The first dimension (equivalent to the internal limit of the assemblage) is the form of content, but it is also known as the *machinic assemblage of bodies*; the second dimension is the form of expression, but it is also known as the *collective assemblage of enunciation*.[25] At its most basic the assemblage combines material 'nondiscursive multiplicities' and expressive 'discursive multiplicities' – one dimension does not map onto the other without remainder, something always escapes. This is because they are dimensions of an active, ongoing process, not a static whole. Deleuze and Guattari's concepts are complex syntheses (meaning one cannot trace back a pure line of derivation, there is always an inexplicable leap) of a range of ideas drawn from a wide variety of sources, so their names change as they evolve and take on board additional components. In this case the name change reflects the combination of Hjelmslev's ideas (form/ content) with that of the Stoics (bodies/attributes) and the work of Leroi-Gourhan (tools/signs).[26] These distinctions cannot be reduced to a simple opposition between things: 'What should be opposed are distinct formalizations, in a state of unstable equilibrium or reciprocal presupposition.'[27]

Although I stated above that the assemblage is a function with (at least) two dimensions, the form of content and the form of expression, this way of putting things is slightly misleading because it obscures the fact that the real work of the assemblage is to bring together a form of content and a form of expression. For convenience we speak of assemblages as already composed things, but what it really names is a state of interactivity between two distinct and autonomous formalizations. These two formalizations are bound together by an assemblage and as an assemblage which *causes* the multiple intensities and singularities captured by the strata to *resonate*, for example, the spear and the desire to use it combined. 'Resonance, or the communication occurring between the two independent orders, is what institutes the stratified system.'[28] Resonance is one of the most important concepts in Deleuze and Guattari's thinking, but it seems largely to have escaped detection and despite the many thousands of words written about Deleuze and Guattari's work almost all commentators – including me, I'm bound to say – give it very little attention. In order to understand what they mean by resonance, which is nowhere fully explained in *A Thousand Plateaus*, we need to turn to *The Logic of Sense*, which is essentially a book about the necessity of resonance. There we learn two things which are crucial to the concept of stratification: first, that it requires an event to bring the two formations into a state of resonance; and second, that resonance – the event – occurs on the expressive side, not the content side. It is the affects and attributes of the expressive formation that resonate and bounce off the bodies on the content side and set them in motion.[29] This is duly reflected in *A Thousand Plateaus* in the concept of the abstract machine, which is the event that gives a stratum its unity (that's why all strata are precisely dated), and the process of deterritorialization, which is effectively the movement of affects as they unite and disunite with bodies. The phalanx would be nothing without the discipline, the courage, the homosocial bonds and the imperial ambition that holds it together; and, these in turn, would never begin to vibrate and bind the group together without being set off by the resonance between several different events – the command to honour the fatherland, the command to honour the family, the command to defend the homeland and so on.

How Does Stratification Work?

In the beginning, there is the chaos of unformed and unstable matters that flow freely as so many mad particles or intensities.[30] This is the *first* of the set of 'first principles' 'The Geology of Morals' alerts us to. They do not specify what types of particles they have in mind, but it soon becomes clear they are referring to every variety of particle imaginable, from specks of sand and dust to the ephemeral kernels of ideas and feelings we call desire. One of the real difficulties of reading this chapter is the fact that it operates on three distinct levels at once – the geological, the organic and the techno-semiological – and only minimally signposts the fact that these three levels are in fact separate domains. This also means that the particles it refers to can be both material and immaterial (a thought or an idea may well be the product of physical processes, but it remains intangible in itself because it lacks an extensive material form), which adds another layer of confusion because it makes it seem that there is no difference in kind between the different types of particles, which is obviously untrue. It is true that Deleuze and Guattari say that semiotic fragments can rub shoulders with chemical interactions, but this is only the case on the plane of immanence and the plane of consistency. And it is only possible because 'they have been uprooted from their strata, destratified, decoded [and] deterritorialized'.[31] It is tempting to think that the geological and organic strata Deleuze and Guattari discuss function as a kind of ramp to work our way up to the techno-semiological stratum, but this would imply that the geological and organic strata are precursors and somehow less evolved or less complex than the techno-semiological model, which they deny, and that the techno-semiological stratum could somehow encompass within it the other two strata, which they also deny. There is no evolution from the geological to the biological to the techno-semiological; one may function as the substratum, or necessary condition for the other, but it is not a sufficient cause of the other. The fact that 'we' humans are organic beings dwelling on a large rock in no way explains what 'we' humans do and ultimately it is what 'we' humans do that is the central focus of schizoanalysis. Neither geology nor biology is our destiny.

This does not mean there is no place for the more-than-human or the other-than-human in Deleuze and Guattari's work. Obviously enough the contrary is true. Deleuze and Guattari were early pioneers of the kind of work in the humanities and social sciences that today focuses on the more-than-human and the other-than-human domains. However, it is also clearly the case that the majority of what Deleuze and Guattari have to say refers only to the techno-semiological stratum. This is simply a fact that can readily be verified by even scantiest of glances at their work. But the deeper theoretical point I want to make here is that we need to keep in mind the fact that because each stratum is differently organized we cannot mobilize the operations of one to explain the workings of another. Rocks don't explain proteins and proteins don't explain identity politics and identity politics don't explain proteins and proteins don't explain rocks. We have to be careful not to fall into the trap of analogy, which is a constant risk with Deleuze and Guattari's work because their terminology seems to push us in that direction, despite their constant warnings against it. The moment we start studying plant biology in order to better understand the rhizomatic meanderings of the mind, we have succumbed to the fallacy of correspondence between strata and engaged in analogical thinking. One stratum may be part of the explanation of what happens on another stratum – there can be no doubt that our physiology (biological stratum) has an effect on our psychology (techno-semiological stratum); our mood is clearly affected by what we eat, by the things we do and indeed by the ground beneath our feet (geological stratum). But that does not mean studying the interactions of blood cells under a microscope can in any way help us to understand mood or any other formation of human desire. Nor does a scientific analysis of the ocean help explain why many of us find it calming to spend time near the sea. The rhizomatic principle that everything can and should be related does not mean that everything *is* related in the same way or more importantly on every plane. Moreover, it is only on the plane of immanence and the plane of consistency that everything can be related.

As we move from the geological and biological strata to the techno-semiological, we move from a swirling soup of material particles to a swirling soup of immaterial particles, or intensities. Intensities go by many names in Deleuze and Guattari's work – for example, affects and becomings are the two most important – but they all have one thing in common: they lack extension. Unlike the other varieties of particles I have mentioned, they do not have a tangible, material, thing-like or object form, or a proper name like love or hate. Intensities are the agitations of the mind and body (for the want of a better way of putting it) that move us in an emotional, spiritual or libidinal sense but we cannot name; they are the stirrings in our mental equilibrium that come before love and hate, anger and frustration; they are the sensations we long to sustain when we're on a 'high' and cannot wait to escape or extinguish when we're stuck feeling 'low'. Deleuze and

Guattari refer to the universe of these nameless agitations of the mind and body as the earth (but also the body without organs and the plane of immanence), but it is perhaps simpler to see it for what it really is, namely a spatialized image of desire in its pure state. This is not the desire of individuals, or even of groups of individuals. It lacks all such specificity. It is desire in general. Desire as it flows through all of us, that is simultaneously more than us, and 'us' at our constitutive core. It is desire conceived as plenitude not lack. It is a formulation of desire that needs to be understood in terms of the things it is capable of creating, and not (as Lacanian psychoanalysis would have it) as a drive towards objects it can never obtain. Desire creates by creating assemblages. These assemblages may become so 'naturalized' that we forget they are assemblages and mistake them for the primary functioning of desire, as is the case with Freud's Oedipal complex and Lacan's notion of lack. But as Deleuze and Guattari demonstrate in *Anti-Oedipus*, both of these models of desire presuppose what they should explain. Desire in its free state has the potential to be destructive, to carry us away or drop us in a black hole, so we need to interrupt it, capture it, manage it and put it to work.

The *second* 'first principle' which follows directly from the *first* 'first principle' is this: 'There simultaneously occurs upon the earth a very important, inevitable phenomenon that is beneficial in many respects and unfortunate in many others: stratification.'[32] Stratification is the process which consists in 'giving form to matters' by 'imprisoning intensities or locking singularities into systems of resonance and redundancy' and thereby creating molecules on the body of the earth. This is, then, the core presupposition upon which the entire schizoanalytic project rests. *Desire is a free flowing stream of intensities subject to processes of capture and coagulation which give rise to and constitute the entire world.* Stratification is the process whereby the apparent 'nothing' of chaotic particles circulating without order becomes the evident 'something' that is life as we know it, with all that entails. The concept of stratification is obviously borrowed from geology, but we should not assume that means Deleuze and Guattari are proposing a geological explanation of everyday life. It is not simply vibrant matter. Stratification borrows two key ideas from a thoroughly destratified version of geology, both of which should be borne in mind as we navigate Deleuze and Guattari's deployment of this concept. First, that we can and should separate the world into distinct 'layers' (we might just as accurately say 'phyla') according to the origin of their formation, that is, not everything happens at the same time, things have a beginning and an end, and while one thing may precede another it is not necessarily its precursor or progenitor; second, that we can and should inquire into the variations that occur both between and within 'layers' ('phyla'), but we should not assume these variations follow a prescribed pattern or plan. Layers imply both the convergence of matter over time and just as crucially the prolonged absence of (or resistance to) processes of disruption and divergence. As such, stratification is ultimately a problem of consistency: How are the strata formed and what holds them together?[33]

As we've seen, Deleuze and Guattari stipulate that there are three main classes of strata (in Hjelmslev's sense): geological, biological and the techno-semiological. The latter breaks down into multiple sub-classes of strata, of which three are particularly important: the organism, significance and subjectification. In actual fact, though, there is no limit to the final number of strata so long as one is able to satisfy two essential requirements: (1) demonstrate the unity and logic of composition and (2) define the limits of the composition, that is, where it begins and where it ends.[34] In geology this is straightforward as any core sample drawn from the earth can readily attest, providing there hasn't been a major geological disturbance (e.g. earthquake, glaciation, volcanic eruption etc.) the layers of rock formed at different periods of the earth's history will be clearly distinct. But it is much less straightforward on the other strata. On the techno-semiological strata, for instance, the lines of separation will tend to be blurry (e.g. surrealism, modernism and postmodernism). Deleuze and Guattari also stipulate that there is no implied hierarchy or order of development in the relation between the three main classes of strata, or indeed any of the strata that we may adduce. The first refers to the formation of the physical geography of the earth itself, specifically the transformation of sediment into rock by means of aggregation, heat or compression; the second refers to the formation of organic life, the transformation of single-cell organisms into the amazing range of complex creatures that populate the earth today; and the third refers to the formation of socialized life, which largely though not exclusively means human society. This is why we don't really need to sweat the science – neither of the first two classes of strata involves socialized life, therefore neither are amenable to philosophical inquiry or analysis in their own terms. Not only that, the mechanism that Deleuze and Guattari put together to explain the process of stratification is drawn from linguistics and not either geology or biology.

Any philosophy we might generate concerning the geological or biological strata is inescapably of a different order from the techno-semiological stratum; it can only ever be a philosophy of what sentient life forms happen to think and feel about these orders of being. As Deleuze and Guattari put it, science is 'the translation of all the flows, particles, codes, and territorialities of the other strata into a sufficiently deterritorialized system of signs, in other words, into an overcoding specific to language.'[35] The three strata differ in terms of their organization, so while there is a movement of matter between the strata the schema of one stratum cannot be used to explain another (the steady accretion of sediment into rock can in no way explain human society, except in some vague metaphorical or analogical manner). Neither the geological nor the biological strata can be used to explain the functioning of the techno-semiological stratum because their capture and coagulation processes are quite different. If they use rhizomes (biological) to explain certain types of psychological behaviour (techno-semiological) they do so by extracting – that is, destratifying – several of this particular plant variety's traits, specifically the way it can branch or put down roots from any part of its body, and using them in a new way. There is however no correspondence between rhizomes as it is understood in plant biology and as it is used in Deleuze and Guattari's psychology. A detailed study of the life cycle of ginger or turmeric is not going to tell us anything meaningful about schizophrenia; likewise a detailed study of schizophrenia is not going to tell us anything meaningful about the life cycle of ginger or turmeric. This may seem obvious when it's put like this, but there is an amazing amount of work in the secondary literature on Deleuze and Guattari that follows precisely this analogical principle.

The difference between each of the strata is a difference of kind, not degree. The step change between them means the three strata are literally incomparable, except in the extremely abstract sense that Deleuze and Guattari approach it. The key difference between them is this: whereas the geological and biological strata are spatial in their organizational make-up, the techno-semiological is spatial *and* temporal. In contrast to the genetic code, for instance, language is superlinear not linear; it can also emit, receive, comprehend and translate code, which the genetic code cannot.[36] 'The temporal linearity of language expression relates not only to a succession but to a formal synthesis of succession in which time constitutes a process of linear overcoding and engenders a phenomenon unknown on the other strata: *translation*, translatability, as opposed to the previous

inductions [geological] and transductions [organic].[37] The meaning
of a phrase or sentence cannot be arrived at additively; one cannot
simply add the meanings of individual words together to arrive at the
meaning of the whole. As anyone who has tried to learn a new language
knows, the meanings of individual words are not a reliable guide to
the meaning of a phrase or sentence because the sequence of words
plays a determining role in which meanings are mobilized. And one
cannot know the meaning of a sentence or phrase until one has heard
it in its entirety. We may be able to guess where a sentence is going – as
autocorrect and autofill on our smart phones try to do, with varying
degrees of success – but even allowing for the built-in redundancies
of syntax and grammar we cannot know with absolute certainty
where it will end up. What we call wit is simply an exploitation of
this aspect of language – the surprise ending, the surprise twist, pun,
juxtaposition or word substitution are all possible because meaning
is superlinear not linear. For this reason, on the techno-semiological
stratum expression is independent of both content and substance,
which is not the case for the other strata. Similarly, translation is only
possible on the techno-semiological stratum.

This brings me to the *third* 'first principle', which is this:
stratification is a process of capture which works by means of coding
and territorialization (the dual processes of the assemblage). Again
they draw on Hjelmslev here in order to construct a working diagram
of the capture and coagulation processes intrinsic to stratification.
Stratification has two basic processes (which are themselves dual
processes) that happen in succession, a first articulation followed
by a second articulation to use Deleuze and Guattari's terms (first
and second remain relative terms). The *first articulation* is a twofold
process consisting of the selection of particles from the great flux
out of which everything forms and the imposition of a statistical
order upon that selection. The *second articulation* depends upon this

process and brings about a further twofold transformation by turning the selected and ordered particles into stable structures. Borrowing from Hjelmslev, they categorize the first articulation as the form of content and the second articulation as the form of expression. The form of expression serves as the basis for what Deleuze and Guattari define as 'relative invariance'.[38] Here one might think of music – at its origin, music was first of all the selection of a highly specific variety of sounds and an ordering of those sounds into notes and chromatic scales (form of content). But it really only becomes music as we understand it (i.e. subject to the law of relative invariance) when these notes and scales are in turn used as the building blocks to create complex compound sounds, that is, sounds that do not occur in nature and cannot occur by accident (form of expression). A comparison between Chinese, Indian, European and Persian music suffices to illustrate that the double articulation process is capable of producing considerable variety (hence relative invariance), despite the apparent simplicity of the process. It also shows we can speak of the emergence of structures without implying evolution.

But, as Deleuze and Guattari are fond of saying, things are even more complicated than this. 'Since every articulation is double, there is not an articulation of content *and* an articulation of expression – the articulation of content is double in its own right and constitutes a relative expression within content; the articulation of expression is also double and constitutes a relative content within expression.'[39] This means there are intermediate states between content and expression, which form the filigree of any given stratum. If we return (briefly) to the example of music the necessity of this doubling of double articulation will become clear. The selection of sounds that constitutes the form of content contains within it an implied principle of relative invariance inasmuch as the sounds chosen conform to an identifiable principle of selection (e.g. the chromatic scale). A particular sequence of sounds emerges and seemingly of itself begins to determine which sounds can be included and which sounds will be excluded (redundancy). This is what Deleuze and Guattari mean when they say something becomes machinic. It has taken on a logic of its own, one that emerges with the selections themselves but then becomes autonomous. The tonic gaps built into the chromatic scale are instances of the content functioning as expression. By the same token, the form of expression of music implies instances of expression, that is, relative invariance, functioning as content in relation to another dimension of the form of expression. In a piece of music a certain refrain may be taken up by a larger or more complex pattern of music and steadily transformed, as happens in certain forms of call and response songs. The second phrase, the response, captures a part of the first phrase, but then transforms it, takes it in a new direction, without ever leaving the original phrase behind. The first may be a solo part and the second choral, they may even sing exactly the same tune, but the additional voices change the timbre and give it a new affect.

There is a *fourth* 'first principle' that I need to address. 'There is a single abstract machine that is enveloped by the stratum and constitutes its unity. This is the Ecumenon, as opposed to the Planomen of the plane of consistency.'[40] The abstract machine is an amphibious concept; it simultaneously constitutes the unity of composition of the stratum and constructs 'continuums of intensity' on the plane of consistency.[41] Assemblages are required to effectuate abstract machines.[42] When 'assemblages fit together the variables of a stratum as a function of its unity, they also bring about a specific effectuation of the abstract machine as it exists outside the strata.'[43] The abstract machine constitutes the diagram of the assemblage.[44] 'The abstract machine is always singular, designated by the proper name of a group or individual. ... The abstract machine does not exist independently of the assemblage, any more than the assemblage functions independently of the machine.'[45] But this makes it seem like the abstract machine is an idealized form, when in fact it is very much a pragmatic concept. Staying with music for a moment, if one thinks about the difference between Chinese, Indian, European and Persian music and tries to quantify it in some way, what one ends up with is a kind of diagram, precisely in the sense Deleuze and Guattari use it. There are a set of rules relating to the invariable elements of each of these musical traditions which cannot be broken without the music starting to sound like something other than what it is traditionally supposed to sound like. But there are also free-floating elements in each tradition which can be captured by other traditions and incorporated without contravening the dictates of the tradition. This is how innovation enters the system and steadily brings about change. It is like the moment when Bob Dylan started using electric guitars and people thought it was the end of folk music, but it was only the end of folk music as it had been understood until then. The essentials remained the same.

Our approach to the abstract machine, as Deleuze and Guattari map it out in the chapter on the novella in *A Thousand Plateaus*, should be to ask one very simple but powerful question: 'Whatever could have happened for things to come to this?'[46] The 'this' in this equation, however, isn't so much a state of affairs as a new reality, either extant or yet to come. For Deleuze and Guattari the classic examples of what they mean by abstract machines are to be found in Kafka's short stories, of which the most typical are the writing machine in 'The Penal Colony', Odradek in 'The Cares of a Family Man' and the bouncing balls in 'Mr Blumfeld, an Elderly Bachelor'. Contrary to their usual habit, Deleuze and Guattari do not deny or negate the standard readings of Kafka which attach allegoric, metaphoric and symbolic meaning to these machines. However, in their view, this way of reading the texts only represents one side of these abstract machines, which also have a 'nonfigurative, nonsignifying, nonsegmental' side to them as well.[47] 'The abstract machine crops up when you least expect it, at a chance juncture when you are just falling asleep, or into a twilight state or hallucinating, or doing an amazing physics experiment. ... There is nothing to explain, nothing to interpret.'[48] These machines are ambivalent; they can push the assemblage towards a closed-up transcendent formation or open it out onto an unlimited field of immanence. The latter option is implicitly coded by Deleuze and Guattari as preferable, even desirable in itself, whereas the former is coded as problematic and decidedly undesirable.

Deleuze's late essay 'Immanence: A Life' is essentially a meditation on this point – *a* life, for Deleuze, is nothing other than this unlimited field of immanence.[49] It is the first closed-up form which prompts the question, *whatever could have happened for things to come to this?* The second form, however, because of its openness, often passes unnoticed, hence Deleuze's interest in it. But we only have to think of the difference between saying to oneself 'I can't do this' and 'I can do this' to know that the second form is just as potent as the first, even if our experience of it tends to be unremarked (except of course in those moments in life when we've been able to transform the former into the latter). If one wanted to give a name to the complicated set of interlocking 'reasons' why one 'can't' do something, then in Deleuze and Guattari's terms it would be the abstract machine. It is a machine because it 'works' – meaning it influences our behaviour – and it is abstract because it has no material or tangible form. Often we don't know it is there, even when it is working, until much later, perhaps only when it is already too late. As Fitzgerald writes, 'I saw that for a long time I had not liked people and things, but only followed the rickety old pretense of liking. I saw that even my love for those closest to me was become only an attempt to love, that my casual relations – with an editor, a tobacco seller, the child of a friend, were only what I remembered I *should* do, from other days.'[50] But as acute as Fitzgerald's self-analysis is, and it is indeed a rare and beautiful piece of introspection, one cannot but sense a certain feeling of helplessness to explain how things had come to this. Hence Deleuze and Guattari's question, the form of which is very precise: *whatever could have happened for things to come to this?* The assumption is that one's own actions did not directly cause the situation in which one finds oneself, or if they did, there was no intention to cause what happened. Somehow it just happened, behind one's back, so to speak. Like becoming an alcoholic, or destroying one's talent, to continue the Fitzgerald examples, these things don't happen because one intends them to happen, but nonetheless they happen because of what one does and because one does not do anything to prevent them from happening.

Why Did They Need the Concept of Stratification?

Why did Deleuze and Guattari need the concept of stratification? There are, I think, four answers to this question. *First*, it means that assemblages produce something other than themselves. If we look closely at their discussion of language, we notice two things that are fundamental to understanding Deleuze and Guattari's version of assemblage theory: (1) language is capable of giving rise to assemblages, but it isn't one itself; (2) language presupposes an assemblage, which is not given in language.[51] Assemblages are not defined by their components; they are defined, rather, by what they produce, and what they produce, ultimately, are the complex forms and objects that populate contemporary society.

My *second* answer is that stratification is needed to begin to analyse and explain the fact that everyday life is experienced by most people as multi-layered, without necessarily being organized or interconnected. Not every layer of our lives connects directly with every other layer of our lives; moreover, we're often sandwiched between layers that we can't even see, much less articulate. Our layers are multi-layered! Our jobs – to take only one example – are not simply one kind of experience. We engage with machines, we engage with people, we engage with command structures and schedules, and a whole host of other kinds of inputs and variables, some of which we can control but most of which is out of hands. In my own career I have seen the emergence of digital technology as a staple of academic life, from the moment when email became the standard form of conducting all communication to the introduction of e-books in libraries and the widespread uptake of pre-recorded online lectures. This in turn has changed the way students read, the way they feel about their presence in the classroom and the way they write and think. I cannot say which of these changes have been 'for the better' and which have been 'for the worse' because the answer depends on so many variables. For example, I prefer to read books on paper, but I appreciate and benefit from the convenience of e-books. My students benefit from the convenience of viewing lectures online according to their personal schedule rather than my or the university's schedule. The changes have been so profound on so many levels that I often wonder whether the career I have now can really be said to be the same one I began when I finished my PhD. The more interesting and much less maudlin response, though, would be to ask whether any new assemblages have appeared. Is a lecture online different in kind to one viewed 'live' in a lecture theatre? Is an e-book different in kind to one made from trees?

This brings me to the *third* answer I want to give, which is that stratification is a periodizing concept. All strata, via the abstract machine they encapsulate (as its unifying principle), are named and dated. The resulting conception of history is not so much non-linear as discontinuous. When geologists and archaeologists dig through the layers, they treat each one as indicating that a particular period in history ended and was succeeded by another. Obviously this does not preclude the particles or components of one historically extinct stratum from continuing to function in the next stratum – neither racism, nor slavery, nor even the enforced migration of peoples ended with the abolition of slavery, but they did take on new forms. As Melinda Cooper shows, when slavery ended in the United States following the Civil War many newly freed slaves were obliged to enter into debt peonage arrangements because they lacked the wherewithal to support themselves and their families.[52] Thus, as one form of slavery ended another began, but its formal structure had changed. Now, putatively free people 'voluntarily' entered into arrangements that previously they were forcibly coerced into entering – the bonds of debt simply replaced the manacles of iron, with the same effect, forcing people to accept unfair, thoroughly exploitative working and living conditions, as well as profound restrictions on their mobility. The same model continues to be used by human traffickers and sweatshops today.

The *fourth* answer I want to give is that if subjects are produced, not given, as Deleuze and Guattari argue, then a process capable of producing subjects and subjectivity must be theorized. This is made clear in the chapter on the body without organs, which introduces three classes of strata not even mentioned in 'The Geology of Morals'. 'Let us consider the great strata concerning us, in other words, the ones that most directly bind us: the organism, significance, and subjectification. The surface of the organism, the angle of significance and interpretation, and the point of subjectification or subjection. You will be organized, you will be an organism, you will articulate your body – otherwise you're just depraved.'[53] The crucial word here is *bind*. At almost every turn in Deleuze and Guattari's work socially binding processes are painted as unfortunate, undesirable, unendurable, and the secondary literature on their work has tended to follow suit, thus turning their work into a kind of anti-repression manifesto. But this shows a lack of appreciation for the way Deleuze and Guattari mobilize free indirect discourse in their writing. We should be asking – following Deleuze's instructions in his essay 'The Method of Dramatization' – for whom is stratification unendurable? The answer to that, perhaps obviously, is schizophrenics; they find stratification unendurable. By contrast, 'we' non-schizophrenics would find the completely unbound existence of the psychotic state absolutely terrifying. However, from time to time, 'we' non-schizophrenics also find suffocating the various social obligations that bind us to our strata and we begin to long for and eventually plan for our escape.

Deleuze and Guattari often say that escaping from the closed-in world of certain types of strata, a process they refer to as destratification, is a good and necessary thing, but they are also very careful to say that too much (or too rapid) destratification can be deadly. If 'you blow apart the strata without taking precautions, then instead of drawing the plane [of immanence] you will be killed, plunged into a black hole, or even dragged toward catastrophe.'[54] That is why Deleuze and Guattari say stratification is both beneficial *and* unfortunate. It depends both on one's perspective and one's situation. Without stratification 'we' could not function as a society – language, tradition, culture, custom and so on are all forms of stratification; but, by the same token, there are aspects of our society that not all of us find equally beneficial. Indeed, some people may even experience some of these things as toxic – we have names for these toxic elements, such as racism, sexism, bigotry and so on. But as much as we may wish never to have to suffer from these toxic aspects of stratification, it is a step too far to say we would be better off if we had never been stratified in the first place. Without stratification there would be no 'we'. Without stratification there would be no 'I'. Without stratification we could not communicate with one another, nor even live together in anything like a society. This tension between that which we cannot live without and that which we cannot live with is central to a great deal of social theory – the key difference, which I'll return to, is this: for Deleuze and Guattari, there is no aspect of human society, no matter how violent and inhumane it may be, that isn't a product of desire. As they have famously insisted, at a certain point and under very specific conditions people desired fascism – they weren't duped into following Hitler, they desired everything he stood for. That, they say, is what really needs to be accounted for, what they call a perversion of desire.[55]

If at this point we look up from the page and think about the world beyond Deleuze and Guattari, we start to wonder at least a couple of things about the concept of stratification. Perhaps most obviously, one wonders whether stratification, as Deleuze and Guattari use the term, bears any resemblance to its more well-known deployments in social theory (e.g. Weber). Does stratification refer to such distinctions as those made by sociology between social classes (poor, middle-class, wealthy and so on), races (black, white etc.), genders (men, women, trans, other), or even more global distinctions such as those between the north and the south? The short answer is no; these kinds of distinctions are covered by another concept, namely segmentarity. The slightly longer answer is that their deployment of stratification is not entirely inconsistent with its usage in social theory (understood very broadly), but it is more abstract – the cuts it makes are between strata that are in effect the preconditions for the kinds of layering of the social world we map by concepts like class, race and gender. Also, stratification is not strictly speaking a sociological concept for Deleuze and Guattari. There are non-human strata as well. While I tend to think one needs to be careful in how one thinks about the relationship between non-human and human strata, it is nevertheless a powerful way of conceptualizing our relationship as humans to our natural environment, something that is becoming increasingly important as climate change begins to make its effects more acutely felt. We as humans have to recognize and take account of the fact that our lives are possible only because of the substrata our planet has yielded to us in the form of our genetic heritage and the sustenance we draw from the earth itself.

If stratification does not follow the pattern of its standard use in social theory then why use the term? Again, the very short answer is that it dramatizes the way Deleuze and Guattari think about the ontology of the world. At its most elementary, their ontology consists of a dual system of an organized transcendental plane sitting on top of an unorganized immanent plane. These two planes, which go by many names in Deleuze and Guattari's work, are inseparable – they are each other's limit and each other's condition of possibility (the limit point of organization is disorganization; by the same token, you cannot have disorganization if you do not at least postulate the idea of its opposite). Moreover, there is constant movement between the two planes – one, the plane of organization, constantly stratifies the other; but at the same time, the other one, the plane of immanence, continuously destratifies its opposite number.[56] This oscillation is the essential rhythm of the schizoanalytic project. Neither state of being is desirable for itself; both are a kind of death. Life occurs in the middle. The slightly longer answer is that we – as Deleuze and Guattari frequently insist – are always in the middle of things – our job, our love life, our interests, our passions and so on – such that any attempt to grasp contemporary life must find some way to take account of the way we are gripped (by multiple sets of double pincers, that is, assemblages) on all sides by the things we choose and (as Žižek says) the things we are forced to choose. Deleuze and Guattari are not voluntarists; they don't think one can simply opt out of a difficult situation. Rather, for them, it is always a matter of engineering escapes, of finding the means to build and execute the assemblages one needs to destratify, just a little, and make one's getaway. But we cannot escape everything, all at once, because that too is a kind of death. So we must choose our lines of flight carefully. Whatever we retain after we have made our getaway is our strata: it is the bedrock of our existence.

2

Desire and Machines

Deleuze and Guattari's concept of the assemblage cannot be understood in the absence of their concept of desire. Yet, assemblage theory in virtually every one of its incarnations (there are noble exceptions, to be sure, such as the work of my colleague Marcelo Svirsky[1]) takes the opposite path and as far as possible – even when it isn't theoretically plausible to do so – excludes any consideration of desire, or the passions that animate desire. This not only fails to appreciate what it is that Deleuze and Guattari were actually trying to do in their work, it also hampers our ability to say anything new about the kinds of entities we might want to determine as assemblages. To date assemblage theory has almost exclusively focused on highly specific types of entities, such as cities (Amin), electricity grids (Bennett), laboratories (Latour) and markets (DeLanda), to name but a few key examples, which can be mapped as interlocking systems of things. In each case, though, there is an untenable assumption that it is possible to somehow 'control' for desire and thereby ignore it, or at any rate treat it as a neutral variable that doesn't require separate consideration. (Bennett even goes so far as to say, astonishingly, that desire isn't necessarily the best category 'through which to think about assemblages'.[2]) But if assemblages are simply systems of things, as these and other commentators claim, then why do we need a new concept like the assemblage to deal with them? Why not just stick with the concept of the system? Or, more pointedly, why adopt a concept like the assemblage and gut it of the very thing that animates it and turn it into something less interesting? The assemblage-as-system-of-things approach apparently forgets that the starting point for the invention of the concept of the assemblage is *desire* understood as the basis of all *behaviour* (animal, human and more-than-human).

The assemblage-as-system-of-things approach exemplified by Bennett and DeLanda, among others, assumes that the properties exhibited by a given assemblage are generated by the materials in the assemblage, but for Deleuze and Guattari the opposite is the case. *Desire is primary; it is desire that selects materials and gives them the properties that they have in the assemblage.* This is because desire itself is productive. This is what Deleuze and Guattari mean by materialism: productive desire. 'If desire produces, its product is real. If desire is productive, it can be productive only in the real world and can produce only reality.'[3] Kant, Deleuze and Guattari argue, was one of the first to conceive of desire as production, but he botched things by failing to recognize that the object produced by desire is fully real. (Deleuze and Guattari reject the idea that superstitions, hallucinations and fantasies belong only to the realm of 'psychic reality', as Kant would have it.)[4] The schizophrenic has no awareness that the reality they are experiencing is not the same reality as everyone else's. If they see their long dead mother in the room with them, they do not question whether this is possible or not; they aren't troubled by any such doubts. What they see is for them what is, quite literally. If this Kantian turn seems surprising, it is nevertheless confirmed by Deleuze and Guattari's critique of Lacan, who in their view makes essentially the same mistake as Kant in that he conceives desire as lacking a real object (for which fantasy acts as both compensation and substitute).

Deleuze and Guattari describe Lacan's work as 'complex', which seems to be their code word for useful but flawed (they say the same thing about Badiou). On the one hand, they credit him with discovering desiring-machines in the form of the *objet petit a* (the little o), but on the other hand they accuse him of smothering his discovery under the weight of the Big O.[5] As Žižek is fond of saying, in the Lacanian universe fantasy is not a substitute for reality, it supports reality. This is because reality, as Lacan conceives it, is inherently deficient; it perpetually lacks a real object, and it is this lack which functions as the motor driving desire. So it needs fantasy to complete it, to paper over the gaps and prevent us from coming into contact with the real, which in the Lacanian universe is regarded as too disturbing to be dealt with in its raw state. If desire is conceived this way, as a support for reality, then, as Deleuze and Guattari argue, 'its very nature as a real entity depends upon an "essence of lack" that produces the fantasized object. Desire thus conceived of as production, though merely the production of fantasies, has been explained perfectly by psychoanalysis.'[6] This is not how desire works according to Deleuze and Guattari because it would mean that all desire does is produce imaginary doubles of reality, creating dreamed-of objects to complement absent real objects. This subordinates desire to the objects it supposedly lacks, or needs, thus reducing it to an essentially secondary role. This is precisely what Deleuze was arguing against when he said that the task of philosophy is to overturn Platonism. Nothing is changed by correlating desire with need as psychoanalysis tends to do. 'Desire is not bolstered by needs, but rather the contrary; needs are derived from desire: they are counterproducts within the real that desire produces. Lack is a countereffect of desire; it is deposited, distributed, vacuolized within a real that is natural and social.'[7] This rejection of a central tenet of Lacan confirms what might be termed the neo-Kantian reading of desire because it means that we cannot define desire in a transitive fashion: any attempt to define desire as the desire *for* something immediately puts us back into the realm of lack.

Productive desire cannot be the desire for something it presently lacks, it must produce something. This brings us to the most important twist in Deleuze and Guattari's rethinking of desire: if desire is productive and what it produces is real then desire's productions must be *actual* and not virtual irrespective of whether or not they are tangible in a physical or material sense. When Deleuze and Guattari describe their work as a form of materialism it is because the unconscious, as they conceive it, is productive, not because they emphasize material objects. Referring to the formation of symptoms, such as hallucinations, Deleuze and Guattari write, 'The actual factor is desiring-production'.[8] To which they add the following important clarification: 'The term "actual" is not used because it designates what is most recent [which is its usual meaning in both French and German], and because it would be opposed to "former" or "infantile" [which is how it is used in Freud's texts]; it is used in terms of its difference with respect to "virtual"'.[9] I doubt there is a more important or consequential statement in the whole of Deleuze and Guattari's writings. Its importance becomes clear in the next sentence:

> And it is the Oedipus complex that is virtual, either inasmuch as it must be actualized in a neurotic formation as a derived effect of the actual factor, or inasmuch as it is dismembered and dissolved in a psychotic formation as the direct effect of this same factor.[10]

This is a major reversal of how we are taught to think about the relationship between the actual and the virtual. To actualize the virtual, then, does not mean that something that was previously only notional or imaginary is thereby made concrete and real (an idea turned into a thing, for example); rather, it means that something that was previously only sensual (felt but not thought) is made present to the mind in an active sense (it becomes an object). The actual is that which concerns the mind right now, where concern would mean an active form of attention which could be either conscious or unconscious (what we commonly refer to as 'preoccupation' would be an example of unconscious active attention). 'For, as Bergson shows, memory is not an actual image which forms after the object has been perceived, but a virtual image coexisting with the actual perception of the object.'[11] Freud's biggest mistake, Deleuze and Guattari claim, which demonstrates his failure to understand this point, was to think that the unconscious is constructed in the image of Oedipus, which would mean that the unconscious is merely a shadow theatre for the conscious and not a productive system in its own right. Freud thus mistook the virtual for the actual and vice versa. The problem of the actual and the virtual is central to the entire schizoanalytic project, but as is obvious from the foregoing discussion Deleuze and Guattari's conceptualization of this problematic does not follow any of the expected paths – it is not used in either an ontological or metaphysical sense, but wholly in what must be called a psychological sense. This must be borne in mind if one is not to be led astray by Deleuze and Guattari's often perplexing rhetoric. Synthesizing desire, which is the other word Deleuze and Guattari sometimes use in place of arranging, is then the basic operation performed by the unconscious, or indeed the mind as a whole. There are a number of sub-operations of synthesizing that Deleuze and Guattari consider, but for present purposes it suffices it to say that synthesizing is what the mind does.

It is only when we turn to a consideration of actions – and not just the elaboration of thoughts and ideas – that we can see the full complexity of this claim because now the usual distinction between actual and virtual must be reversed. The physical elements in a given assemblage are not necessarily 'actual' from the point of view of the construction of the assemblage; they are merely the props and as we'll see in the case of Little Joey (Bruno Bettelheim's patient) they aren't always necessary. In this precise sense they should be considered virtual. As an illustration of this point, one can think of the productive relation (well known to capitalism) between children's television and movies and the tie-in toys and merchandise – putting an image of Lightning McQueen on a can of baked beans only works because that image is *actual* for its target audience, that is, kids of a certain age. In the absence of the movie, and more importantly an intimate knowledge and appreciation of the movie, the image is flat and unaffecting, that is, merely virtual. Here I would go a step further and say it is the characters rather than the plot or storyline that matters (obviously these are not strictly separable) inasmuch that children give the characters a life beyond the movie – they don't tend to re-enact scenes from the movie; they create their own scenes based on their understanding of the 'inner life' of the characters they like. This process, it seems to me, is neither one of identification nor emulation but something machinic (i.e. a 'synthesis of heterogeneities'[12]) – the characters are zones of intensity (components of territories in other words) the children pass through rather than identities they pretend to inhabit. This is an important cue to understanding the concept of the assemblage (here it is worth noting that the territory is the first form of the assemblage), which all too often is simply equated with the composition of a set of physical props.

Assemblages have a beating heart, as it were, which means their particular arrangement of things is *necessary* and as the 'Little Joey' case demonstrates it remains in place even when the material things they arrange are removed. By the same token, the children who ask for baked beans because it has an image of Lightning McQueen on the can don't need either those beans or that can to be *invested* in the character. Invest, as Deleuze and Guattari use it, is a translation of the French word *investissement*, which is itself a translation of the German word *Besetzung* that in English is better known by the Greek word *cathexis*. Much to Freud's displeasure, Ernest Jones translated Freud's word, *Besetzung*, which in ordinary English might have been rendered as 'occupation' (in the military sense) with the Greek word for occupation, *cathexis*. In French, *Besetzung* was rendered as *investissement*, which has as one of its meanings 'investment' in a financial sense, but can also mean to encircle or lay siege in a military sense, which is obviously much closer to the German original than finance.[13] However, it seems it is this latter sense – finance – that prevails in Deleuze and Guattari's thinking, as can be seen for instance in their discussion of the surplus value of desire. But a glimmer of its other military meaning is apparent, obviously enough, in the concept of the war-machine. If we think about the child playing out the various Lightning McQueen scenarios they come up with, we can see that both senses apply: on the one hand, they clearly reap a return on the investment of their desire (which Deleuze and Guattari refer to as the surplus value of desire), but on the other hand they are just as clearly preoccupied with and by their game. However, it only works because the Lightning McQueen assemblage is *actual* for them. The whole of capitalism insists that we cash in our fantasies and valorize commodities and substitute little plastic toy cars we can put on a shelf in place of the exhilarating intensities (becomings) we can experience by passing through – not identifying with – the territory that is Lightning McQueen. The toys do not symbolize anything, they are agents of becoming. They help us to enter the territories of our favourite characters and experience the intensities there, but that doesn't make them fetishes. This becoming, however, depends upon the active operation of an assemblage.

The assemblage is an actual *composition of desire* – 'there is no desire but assembling, assembled, desire' [*il n'y a de désir qu'agençant, agencé, machiné*].[14] As the original French indicates more clearly than the translation does, it is desire itself that is *machined* (meaning it functions in a machinic way, that is, it is autonomously productive like the bouncing celluloid balls in the Kafka story 'Mr Blumfeld, an Elderly Bachelor', which are uncanny because they appear unbidden and bounce without any apparent impetus), in the assemblage, not by the assemblage I hasten to add. The machine is not an object of desire. The assemblage does not make desire into a machine. *The assemblage is desire in its machinic modality*. And, what's more, this is the only modality in which it can be apprehended. This is the founding insight of schizoanalysis and it is there in full view in the opening pages of *Anti-Oedipus* – desire is machinic, not Oedipal, they couldn't be clearer or more insistent. They reject Freud's assumption – hypothesis – that Oedipus is the universal truth of desire and argue instead for what they characterize as a materialist or machinic model of desire (Oedipus is just another variety of assemblage). This does not mean, however, that schizoanalysis is in effect a psychoanalysis of machines, or worse a psychoanalysis of material objects such as 'packages of noodles, cars or 'thingumajigs''. They are quite scathing in their dismissal of this possibility, describing it as an 'utterly dreary and dull' prospect.[15] And we need to take care today that we don't turn assemblage theory into that dreary and dull discourse Deleuze and Guattari warned us about by forgetting the centrality of desire as an organizing force. And it is the structure and operation of the organization of desire in its machinic modality that the concept of the assemblages names and maps. The arrangement of physical component parts is just one part of this puzzle and by no means the most important part.

Initially Deleuze and Guattari used the term 'desiring-machine' to try to capture what they wanted to say about the nature of desire, but they quickly abandoned it because it was subject to too many (mis) understandings.[16] People didn't seem to grasp to their satisfaction that it is desire itself that is machinic and though they spoke of a great many different kinds of machines it was never the meshing of cogs and wheels of actual physical machines that interested them, much less the precise variety of the material the cogs and wheels were manufactured from. Yet that has been the direction of much of the recent work in assemblage theory, particularly its vital materialist permutations, and though Deleuze and Guattari's work is usually claimed as an inspiration for the 'material turn', it is in many ways a reversal of their project. Concerning machines, Deleuze and Guattari direct us to ask two interrelated questions: 'Given a certain effect, what machine is capable of producing it? And given a certain machine, what can it be used for?'[17] This may sound relatively straightforward, but if one looks carefully at the example that follows it becomes clear that it is no ordinary kind of machine that they have in mind. '[O]n being confronted with a complete machine made up of six stones in the right-hand pocket of my coat (the pocket that serves as the source of the stones), five stones in the right-hand pocket of my trousers, and five in the left-hand pocket (transmission pockets), with the remaining pocket of my coat receiving the stones that have already been handled, as each of the stones moves forward one pocket, how can we determine the effect of this circuit of distribution in which the mouth, too, plays a role as a stone-sucking machine?'[18] The stones may appear to be the working parts of this particular assemblage, but it is by no means obvious what work they do. We can be sure though that it has little to do with the material properties of the stones themselves – they are props, necessary perhaps, but not efficient causes (in someone else's hands they would not have the same agency). One could easily imagine substituting marbles for rocks and the machine would continue to function just as it had before.

Deleuze and Guattari offer the stones-machine example drawn from Beckett as a refutation of psychoanalysis' methods because it is impossible to say how or where pleasure fits into this equation. However, we can also see it as a refutation of the idea that the assemblage can be understood from the perspective of its material. This is even more apparent in Deleuze and Guattari's discussion of Bettelheim's case study 'Little Joey', about which they say there 'are very few examples that cast as much light on the regime of desiring-production'.[19] As a patient at the Sonia Shankman Orthogenic School in Chicago, which Bettelheim directed for several years, Joey was classified as autistic, although his symptoms seem more consistent with childhood schizophrenia. Joey thought of himself as a machine and he was only 'present', that is, attentive and communicative, when he was connected to 'electricity'. The rest of the time he was silent, virtually catatonic, hence the autistic label. His body needed an energy source to function, so wherever he went he had to be 'plugged in'. Bettelheim describes Joey's routine as follows: 'Laying down an imaginary wire he connected himself with his source of electricity. Then he strung the wire from an imaginary outlet to the dining room table to insulate himself, then plugged himself in. (He had tried to use real wire, but this we could not allow ...) The imaginary electrical connections he had to establish before he could eat, because only the current ran his ingestive apparatus. He performed this ritual with such skill that one had to look twice to be sure there was neither wire nor outlet nor plug.'[20] He had other machines too, such as his sleeping machine, which consisted of an elaborate array of aluminium foil, paper plates and plastic cups. Effectively, he had a different machine for each of the operations he was expected to perform in daily life – breathing, eating, sleeping, bathing, urinating and so on.

This case is instructive for our purposes here because it sheds light on two aspects of the concept of the assemblage that are frequently overlooked. If we look at 'Little Joey's' machines it is obvious that the materials did not and indeed could not function in the way (we assume) he believed they functioned. He was never actually plugged into a live electrical circuit and while it may be wrong to say his circuitry was 'imaginary' as Bettelheim puts it, it would also be wrong to say it was 'real' in any straightforwardly 'realist' sense as well. He was never permitted to use 'real wire' to plug himself into the building's electricity supply, for obvious reasons, and he was similarly prevented from having any actual wire which he could 'pretend' to plug himself in with. Bettelheim was of the view that Joey's fascination with machinery 'ruled out any contact with reality', so his therapeutic strategy focused on gradually weaning him off his machines by removing all his props.[21] He never succeeded in this goal, doubtless because Joey's need for the machines was deep and genuine. Bettelheim's injunction against the use of 'real wire' is telling because it indicates that the specific quality of the materials was unimportant. He did not need 'real wire' because his wiring existed in his head. It was anything but 'mind independent' but was still very real. It powered and sustained him and he felt he couldn't breathe normally without it. When Bettelheim's staff removed the bricolage of foil, paper plates and plastic cups he cobbled together to construct his other machines, those machines continued to function too, without interruption, indicating that their physical manifestation was merely a matter of convenience or appearance but never essential. So while they were real machines for Joey, they were nevertheless not real machines in any conventional 'realist' sense. *Assemblages are not collections of things.* In many cases the physical things assemblages draw into themselves are completely incidental, just so many props needed to actualize a particular *arrangement of desire.*

We get no nearer to an understanding of Joey's assemblage by examining the materials he used to make his machines (what can be said about his imaginary wires?). We have to look instead at what the machines did for him, at the effects they produced, and ask why he needed them. It is the underpinning *organization of desire* that matters, not the bits and bobs, and this is true for all varieties of the assemblage. Joey's case shows that the material components of an assemblage do not by themselves disclose the machinic arrangement of desire it orchestrates. This brings me to the second point I wanted to raise in relation to 'Little Joey'. If desire is all too frequently overlooked in assemblage theory then it is perhaps no surprise that the concept of the body without organs (in any of its guises including the plane of immanence and the plane of consistency) is also – again, all too frequently – overlooked as well because desire *desires* on the body without organs. One cannot speak of desire in Deleuze and Guattari in the absence of their concept of the body without organs just as one cannot speak of the body without organs without taking into account their concept of desire. Deleuze and Guattari's interest in this case stems from what they see as Bettelheim's intuitive appreciation of the agency of what they call the body without organs (which he calls autism) and the innovative treatment he initiates as a consequence. Like Bettelheim, they see Joey as locked-in, caught in a psychic vacuum in which his desiring-machines are spinning endlessly, but without any meshing of the gears, thus offering him no relief from their productions – his psychotic ideations – and no way out of the world they have constructed for him.[22] In its first formulation, this is what the body without organs looked like for Deleuze and Guattari ('eyes closed tight, nostrils pinched shut, ears stopped up'[23]): *desire at degree zero.* In later works they would revise this view of the body without organs and develop an active and affirmative form of it as well.[24] Bettelheim's innovation, which Deleuze and Guattari say he shares with Pankow, is to first of all try to understand Joey's machines for themselves and not see them as some kind of childhood regression;

in recognizing that these machines are in fact the operations of the unconscious at work and not so many satisfactions of unconscious desires – in other words, he treats the machines as ongoing processes rather than desired-objects – he found ways to set them in motion again.[25]

What then is the body without organs? This is a complicated concept made more complicated than it perhaps needs to be by the fact that it evolves in Deleuze and Guattari's work such that one cannot say the body without organs of *Anti-Oedipus* is the same as the body without organs in *A Thousand Plateaus*. Matters are not helped by Deleuze and Guattari saying that they aren't even sure if they each meant the same thing by it! We can say with certainty, though, contra Jane Bennett, that the body without organs is not an assemblage.[26] As a matter of conceptual logic, it cannot be an assemblage. Deleuze and Guattari are very clear about this. 'Are not assemblages necessary to fabricate each BwO, is not a great abstract Machine necessary to construct the plane of consistency?'[27] The assemblage, the body without organs and the abstract machine are all different concepts, each with a different function in the overall schema. They are inextricably interconnected, such that none of them are thinkable in the absence of the other.[28] Bennett defines the body without organs as the 'human body working itself out of its organ-ization as an organic whole' towards what she calls 'self-rehybridization', which is never 'an achieved state'.[29] Again, this is wrong-headed because Deleuze and Guattari are very clear that the body without organs is *not* bodily – one can only reach it via the body (in the fullest sense of that word), but it is not itself bodily and cannot be (after all they say capital, too, is a body without organs). Therefore to say it is a human body is to put us off the scent. A very simple example will illustrate the point. If someone says their heart is broken, one does not imagine that they are in need of a cardiologist; one knows that it is not *that* heart that is the problem. The heart the broken-hearted speak of exists on a different plane to the physical body. It is real, to be sure, and its effects are real too, and its effects may even be felt in the visceral body, but it is not the same heart as the muscular organ that circulates our blood. Fixing this heart requires love, poetry, solitude, companionship, soulful healing and many other things besides, which may or may not pass through the body but are not necessarily bodily. Kind words can heal a broken heart but a heart transplant cannot.

Here one must recall Deleuze and Guattari's interest in the concept of the incorporeal transformation, for that is the realm of the body without organs.[30] The body without organs is the plane of immanence we must presuppose so that a statement like 'I have a broken heart' can make sense. It is the plane of the event of having a broken heart. On this plane anything and everything can mix and intertwine because it is all of the same substance, namely affect (intensity and becoming are its other names). In this regard it perhaps does make sense to equate the body without organs with Bhabha's notion of hybridity (third space), as Bennett suggests, because that also consists of pure affect.[31] But this is not how Bennett conceives of it, as her example of cross-species organ transplants makes abundantly clear.[32] For Bennett, everything moves on a material plane, or must somehow be shown to have a material form, whereas for Deleuze and Guattari this is not the case. Following the Stoics they make a rigorous distinction between the realm of bodies and the realm of attributes – the latter attach to bodies, but they are not themselves bodily. This is why statements like 'I love you' or 'I am broken-hearted' should be understood as incorporeal transformations – they transform us but not in the manner of one body colliding with another. It goes much deeper than that. When someone says 'I love you' the transformation it brings about in you, the recipient, applies to your body, 'but it is itself incorporeal, internal to enunciation.'[33]

This division between the realm of bodies (content) and the realm of attributes (expression) is the basic mechanism of the assemblage, and it demands we draw a hard distinction – which Bennett and others do not – between the intermingling of bodies (as when a knife cuts flesh) and the expressed of statements such as 'a knife cuts flesh', which are incorporeal transformations.[34] The separation of these two registers, content and expression, does not preclude movement between them, but it does preclude any form of parallelism, and any sense that the one represents the other. Expression is not signification, it does not represent bodies – it intervenes in bodies.

The body without organs is not inert, it is an active agency of the mind and – dare I say – of the soul. Even in its defensive mode we should not assume it is passive or inactive. On the contrary, it is actively protecting the subject by walling them in; the trouble is – as with so many attempts at 'self-cure' as Freud called it – this walling-in prevents the subject from making the vital connections they need to sustain themselves. The concept of the rhizome should be understood in this context as the beginnings of a 'self-cure' (if I can use that phrase without us getting too hung up on the word cure, which Deleuze and Guattari are also suspicious of) because it implies that the way out of the walled-in world of the schizo is to be found by following the slenderest of threads out of the labyrinth. If everything can be connected, then we can 'connect' our way out of the dark place by connecting to lighter and lighter thoughts and ideations. Cure here doesn't mean either returned to some mythical pre- or non-ill state, or taken to some equally mythical post- or non-ill state, it means becoming unstuck, getting going again and not spinning one's wheels. The child who picks up their plastic Lightning McQueen toy and zooms it across the floor, the kitchen table, or out of the pram and onto the ground, isn't pretending to be an imaginary character from a movie; they are setting a desiring-machine into motion. The toy car doesn't complete them, it isn't an extension of them, nor does it stand in for anything or anyone – not them or mommy or daddy, and so on (these being the three main ways psychoanalysis gets desiring-machines wrong).[35] The car and the expressive weight of the character Lightning McQueen it resonates with enables the child to experience movement where previously there was stasis.

But it is desire itself that zooms and it zooms on the body without organs, tracing a line of flight across its plateau of possibilities. The toy car, by itself, can tell us nothing of the freight of desire it can be invested with. It is, they argue, contradictory to maintain, as psychoanalysis does (particularly the Kleinian inflected object relations branch of psychoanalysis which also includes Winnicott), that the infant lives among 'partial objects' – that is, objects that attract, or better yet, initiate the child's desiring, such as electrical outlets, the bane of every new parent's existence – and conceive of these objects as representative of the child's parents. Klein, they say, was among the 'least prone to see everything on terms of Oedipus' yet she nevertheless uses it as the 'sole measure of desiring-production' even at the price of enacting a kind of 'terrorism' on her charges, as her account of her interactions with Little Richard cited by Deleuze and Guattari illustrate. She writes, 'I took a big train and put it beside a smaller one *and called them* "Daddy-train" and "Dick-train". Thereupon he picked up the train I called Dick and made it roll to the window and said "Station". *I explained*: "The station is mummy; Dick is going into mummy."'[36] That Dick runs out of the room after this brief exchange doesn't seem to trouble Klein at all, much less interrupt her Oedipalizing flow of interpretations which give the poor boy no way out, nowhere to turn, except towards mummy and daddy. In Deleuze and Guattari's view, the child learns, willingly or not, to relate their desire to their parents, but this is not how things start out. In the beginning, desire flows in all directions. 'A child never confines himself to playing house, to playing only at being daddy-and-mommy. He also plays at being a magician, a cowboy, a cop or a robber, a train, a little car. The train is not necessarily daddy, nor is the train station necessarily mommy.'[37] The magician, the cowboy, the cop and the robber are not daddy either; they are all instances of desire escaping the familial triangle and flowing towards figures drawn from the child's everyday life, most likely their interaction with popular media of some sort (film, TV, comic books and so on).

This does not mean we should dismiss the importance of the parents, Deleuze and Guattari say, but it does mean we should question the assumption that the parents are the primary agents in the formation of the child's desire. Instead of assuming, as psychoanalysis does, that the parents form an inescapable matrix for desire, and that the child's desire can only develop within that matrix, we should be asking how it is that the child does come to regard the parents as 'special agents' of desire. What forces are required to triangulate and close up desire in this way?[38] However, before we can answer this question, which will eventually take us to the gates of the assemblage, we need to first of all ask what the nature of desire is such that it can be captured by such forces as are deployed by Oedipus. It is worth bearing in mind, at this point, that when Guattari was asked to supply a definition of assemblage for a glossary appended to the English translation of *Molecular Revolution* (which somewhat unhelpfully combines sections of two of his books, *Psychanalyse et transversalité* (1972) and *La Révolution moléculaire* (1977)) he offered that it replaced the notion of the complex, as in the Oedipal complex.[39] From the outset assemblage was never intended to refer to ensembles of material things. It was always about the organization of desire. Deleuze and Guattari's answer to the question what is the nature of desire such that it can be captured begins to take form in their critique of Klein's account of partial objects. It may not be immediately obvious, particularly not to those readers who skip

Anti-Oedipus and jump straight to *A Thousand Plateaus* in their quest to understand assemblage theory (which still puts them way ahead of those who skip reading primary texts altogether), but the world of partial objects, the 'world of explosions, rotations, [and] vibrations' in which objects of all varieties (mundane, bodily, excremental and so on) excite desire, causing it to flow, is fundamental to assemblage theory.[40]

Klein discovered this world, according to Deleuze and Guattari, but unfortunately failed to grasp its logic. There are two reasons for this failure which, they imply, remain with us today inasmuch that psychoanalysis has not moved beyond either one. First, she treats them as fantasies rather than real processes of production. Second, and in a way more damagingly, she cannot rid herself of the idea that the partial objects must somehow relate to a whole, either an original whole that has been lost or one that will appear later. So although she saw something in her sessions with children that obviously had a powerful life of its own, a mode of desire or better yet desiring that did not answer to any preconceived rules about how desire is stimulated and organized, but seemed on the contrary to have no organization at all, she mapped it all back onto the parents and instead of breaking the shackles of Oedipus she made their grip all the more secure.[41] But, Deleuze and Guattari write, it is contradictory 'to maintain, on the one hand, that the child lives among partial objects, and that on the other hand he conceives of these partial objects as being his parents, or even different parts of his parents' bodies' because to do so is to deprive those objects of the explosive power they clearly possess. Not only that, they say, 'it is not true that a baby experiences his mother's breast as a separate part of her body. It exists, rather, as a part of a desiring-machine connected to the baby's mouth, and is experienced as an object providing a nonpersonal flow of milk, be it copious or scanty.'[42]

Deleuze was already thinking along these lines in 1967, two years before he met Guattari, as his work on masochism shows (which I will discuss in greater detail in the next section). The keenest insight into Deleuze's methods *Masochism* offers is to be found precisely in its counter-intuitive argument against what Deleuze calls the *material dimension of masochism*. Deleuze says if we start from the material content, by which he means the pleasure-pain complex that supposedly underpins masochism, 'we solve everything ... but at the price of total confusion.'[43] This could be a watchword for assemblage theory in general, which is frequently guilty of this particular methodological sin. Even if it is the material dimension of the assemblage which piques our interest, as it frequently is, analysis should not begin there because the material does not disclose its meaning, function – its mattering – by itself. At most, the material dimension can be thought of as a machinic index, which Deleuze and Guattari define as 'the signs of an assemblage that has not yet been established or dismantled because one knows only the individual pieces that go into making it up, but not how they go together.'[44] This is how we should approach all material, as a machinic index, as a sign or collection of signs that an assemblage may be in operation, and as a question mark as to the nature of the assemblage that might give it unity. We should not assume, though, that an assemblage is always to be found; what we encounter may well lack purpose and structure and amount to nothing more than the proverbial 'heap of fragments'.[45] Not everything we encounter is an assemblage, or part of an assemblage – some stones are just stones, even the stones that happen to be in our pockets, just as some cigars are just cigars.

The body without organs isn't always strong or healthy. As we all know, one does not always have the strength to make declarations like 'I love you', 'I am broken-hearted', 'I need help' and so on. Often such poignant expressions go unexpressed, but like so many letters that have not been mailed or have wound up in the dead letter office (Bartelby), that does not mean they disappear, or cease to pulse within us. Indeed, in Deleuze and Guattari's terms, the things we feel we must say but cannot say are 'so many nails piercing the flesh, so many forms of torture'.[46] When Artaud said he wanted to have done with organs, this is what he was referring to, the constant demand to 'say this' and 'do that' which he simply couldn't live up to. A body without organs is, on this formulation which owes as much to Melanie Klein's concept of the liquid object as it does Antonin Artaud's poem, a mechanism of self-defence. 'In order to resist organ-machines, the body without organs presents its smooth, slippery, opaque, taut, surface as a barrier. In order to resist linked, connected, and interrupted flows, it sets up a counterflow of amorphous, undifferentiated fluid.'[47] In *Anti-Oedipus*, the body without organs is associated with both autism and catatonia and is generally treated as a symptom of a breakdown, meaning the loss of the capacity to act. But one can already see a flicker of the more affirmative version of it that emerges in *A Thousand Plateaus* in their account of the development of paranoia. 'This is the real meaning of the paranoiac machine: the desiring-machines attempt to break into the body without organs, and the body without organs repels them, since it experiences them as an over-all persecution apparatus.'[48] At first glance this may not seem particularly affirmative, but the point not to be missed here is that the body without organs functions not just as a mechanism of defence but also – and much more importantly – as a *power of selection*. The body without organs is positioned here as an agency of the mind that determines when and how and under what conditions desire can flow. In *Anti-Oedipus*, when the conditions are not optimal, the body without organs shuts down and retreats into itself, causing all the flows of desire to cease, hence the connection to autism and catatonia. However, in *A Thousand Plateaus* Deleuze and Guattari introduce an important modification to their concept to allow for the possibility that the body without organs can be consciously modified, either by the subject themselves or another party such as the therapist. That is why they ask the question, how do you make yourself a body without organs?

The Masochist Assemblage

Assemblages differ from one another at the level of their form, not their content. Indeed, it is perfectly possible for assemblages to have the same content and still differ from one another, which is effectively Deleuze's argument against the notion of sadomasochism.[49] We can take it further and say that other types of fiction, such as fantasy fiction and historical romances, to name only the most obvious, sometimes contain elements that are recognizably sadistic or masochistic in origin or influence (e.g. scenes of sexual violence and fetishist costuming), but that does not mean they should be placed in the same category as either Sade or Masoch. Readers of fantasy fiction and historical romances will not necessarily enjoy reading Sade or Masoch, and they probably wouldn't even be interested in Sade or Masoch because their own tastes are elsewhere. If the content is ambiguous, as these examples suggest very strongly it is, then one must look elsewhere for a properly differential diagnosis. Deleuze's argument in *Masochism*, and all his subsequent work, is that these differences must be traced to the formal structure of the assemblage, its forms of content and its forms of expression. We need, he says, 'a genuinely formal, almost deductive psychoanalysis which would attend first of all to the formal patterns underlying the processes, viewed as formal elements of fictional art.'[50] The significance of this statement cannot be overestimated because it goes to the heart of Deleuze's project: what he refers to here as an underlying formal pattern is the abstract machine. When Deleuze reads Masoch, his goal is *to uncover the architecture* (diagram) of the 'real that is yet to come' (abstract machine) implicit in his work. He approaches the work like a detective, asking at every turn 'whatever could have happened for desire to work in this way?' He deduces the architecture of Masoch's abstract machine by focusing on four aspects of his work: (1) language, (2) ontology, (3) mechanism (or device) and (4) fantasy. What he shows is that sadism and masochism are distinct 'realities' (not only distinct from each other but distinct from 'other' realities as well), with their own constitutive rules, and not simply sexual mores.

It is Masoch's style that draws Deleuze's attention; he sees in it the makings of a great work of symptomatology, which he says is why Masoch's name is remembered today. He was the first to draw the diagram of the assemblage that as a result bears his name. It is worth adding here that Deleuze and Guattari say all abstract machines bear the names of the inventors, as masochism does.[51] Masoch's work is interesting and something more than an empty exercise in soft-core pornography (Deleuze says it is deserving of the more exalted classification 'pornology') because it diagrams *a new type of reality*. Deleuze will later say that it isn't necessarily a good or better reality, but that is beside the point because it constitutes a new and distinctive way of being in the world. Although his first work on Masoch, the short book *Masochism: Coldness and Cruelty* published in 1967 (a few years before he met Guattari), remains largely psychoanalytic in its approach, it is evident he was already beginning to formulate his ideas in such a way that one can understand why he felt the need to invent (with Guattari's help) the 'holy trinity' of concepts familiar to us from his later work. His second and third instalments on masochism produced with Guattari (in *Kafka: Toward a Minor Literature* and *A Thousand Plateaus* respectively) eschew any mention of psychoanalysis, except to say psychoanalysis gets masochism all wrong, but do not disavow any aspect of the first iteration of his engagement with Masoch. This could be read in several different ways, of course, but in my view it suggests two things: that Deleuze considered the first book to be sufficiently removed from traditional forms of psychoanalysis that he did not feel the need to disavow it (as he did his first publications, which he came to regard as too theological) and that there was enough in the first book that 'stood up' even if one were to ignore the psychoanalytic dimensions of it.

Deleuze and Guattari's writing on masochism shows in outline form the development of their thought as an intervention into behavioural studies, culminating in what we know today variously as either assemblage theory or schizoanalysis. In the first instalment, *Masochism*, one sees the abstract machine taking shape as the name that will be given to what might be thought of the compulsive feeling that the masochist has that things need to be this way and not any other. In the second and third instalments we see the concept of the body without organs integrated into their methodology. This is not, however, the only point of interest in Deleuze and Guattari's work on Masoch. It also highlights two key elements of their methodology that are often overlooked: (1) it is deductive, it isn't interested in surface phenomena, it wants to expose underlying patterns (not to be confused with 'depth'); (2) it is not materialist, if by that one means it gives priority to the material dimension of that which it encounters. On the contrary, Deleuze and Guattari are quite explicit that to their minds the expressive dimension (the territory or T-factor) always comes first, because it is that which causes matter to matter. It is, I think, a misnomer to call Deleuze and Guattari new materialists; it would be more accurate and perhaps more useful to call them *expressive materialists*. It is the form of expression that gives shape to the form of content. 'The enunciation [form of expression] precedes the statement [form of content], not as a function of the subject that would have produced it but as a function of the assemblage that makes this into its first gear in order to connect to other gears.'[52] This proposition, which is drawn from Deleuze and Guattari's book on Kafka, is central to their work as a whole.

This is why Deleuze says clinicians do not pay enough attention to the actual texts of Sade and Masoch and overhastily latch onto the material elements – the whips, chains and the giving and receiving of pain – when the real crux of the matter is to be found elsewhere. We've been told so many times that sadism and masochism are to be found in the same person (as though they were simply erotic tastes that varied with mood and personality type and not abstract machines embedded in assemblages), he says, that it feels as though we have to believe it.[53] This should make us suspicious. If something is only true, or rather only feels true, because it has been repeated like an advertisement, then the chances are this is because it lacks proper philosophical foundation. And that is precisely what Deleuze wants to argue is the case with the concept of sadomasochism, which in his view is very poorly formed because it relies on several false assumptions about the nature of sadism and masochism. The exclusive focus on the giving and receiving of pain, by psychoanalysis as well as philosophy, is the key problem for Deleuze. He likens it to a doctor treating a fever 'as though it were a definite symptom of a specific disease', which is something no doctor would do because fevers are 'common to a number of possible diseases'.[54] That, he says, is 'surely to proceed by abstraction'.[55]

We are told that some individuals experienced pleasure both in inflicting pain and suffering it. We are told furthermore that the person who enjoys inflicting pain experiences in his innermost being the link that exists between the pleasure and the pain. But the question is whether these 'facts' are not mere abstractions, whether the pleasure-pain link is being abstracted from the concrete formal conditions in which it arrives.[56]

This passage is important because, as Deleuze goes on to clarify, it shows that what he objects to philosophically in the various accounts of sadomasochism produced by psychoanalysis is the assumption 'that there is an underlying common "substance" which explains in advance all evolutions and transformations'.[57] In agreement with Marx's famous inversion of Hegel, Deleuze always advocates that analysis should proceed from the concrete to the abstract, and not the other way around.[58] But this does not mean one should thereby start with the material dimension, as though it were a concrete given. Deleuze is fine with abstraction – indeed, as he and Guattari say in *A Thousand Plateaus*, the only danger presented by processes of abstraction is when one isn't abstract enough – but it must be arrived at by properly critical means and not presupposed, either objectively or subjectively. This has two crucial implications that underpin the development of the concept of the assemblage: first, desire is not an undifferentiated substance; second, desire can only manifest in assemblages. Assemblages have in common the fact that they are all arrangements of desire, but this does not mean that desire is the same in every assemblage, nor does it mean that all assemblages arrange desire in the same way or that they all have the same components. Differentiating and evaluating the different forms of assemblage that one encounters is an essential task of the larger project Deleuze and Guattari refer to as schizoanalysis. All individual assemblages are *formally different* from one another; they are all arrangements of desire, to be sure, but as Deleuze insists is the case with masochism and sadism, they are not necessarily arranged in the same way.

Deleuze proposes that Sade and Masoch eroticize language itself. That is to say, it isn't the content of the writing that is erotic, though doubtless some people may experience it as such; rather language itself is an indispensable element *in* the writing and thus to both assemblages. ('Everything must be stated, promised, announced and carefully described before being accomplished.'[59]) Sade's libertines in *120 Days of Sodom* derive their satisfaction not so much from the sexual acts they carry out as from the fact that they do so in accordance with the words of the storytellers. In this way, word becomes the law and the law itself is perverted.[60] Similarly, Masoch's heroes go to great lengths to put in writing precisely what they expect and want of their chosen tormenters and even go so far as to set it all out in a contract so that their words are followed to the letter. In contrast to Sade's libertine 'instructors', however, Masoch's heroes are 'educators' and 'persuaders'. They have to find, seduce and train their tormenters. So while Masoch's language is spruced with imperatives, as Sade's is, the wellspring of these instructions is something that one would never find in Sade, namely a consensual agreement between the parties as to their respective roles.

In Sade language is demonstrative; it signals the matchless power of the author and his many mouthpieces over his (their) world. Sade's libertines are all immensely talkative, indeed many do nothing but talk, and they constantly expound theories about the way things are, which in their world is always identical with the way things should be. But as Deleuze points out, despite all their proselytizing they are not interested in persuading anyone to their way of seeing things. On the contrary, nothing would be more alien to the sadist than persuasion because it would indicate that their outlook isn't as singular as they supposed. The sadist wants to 'demonstrate that reasoning itself is a form of violence, and that he is on the side of violence, however calm and logical he may be. ... The point of the exercise is to show that the demonstration is identical to violence.'[61] This is why obeying the demands of the storytellers is, paradoxically enough, a highly sadistic act. The libertine's demands are ruthlessly objective, mathematical even, taking into account neither the pleasure (potential or otherwise) of the torturer nor the actual suffering of the victims, which is very often quite considerable.[62] Sade's heroes are apathetic – they are repelled by enthusiasm (they neither love what they do nor hate the ones they do it to). They do what they do coldly, without concern for consequences (good or bad, for themselves or for their victims). And take their pleasure from a deliberate negation of the ego.[63] 'The acts of violence inflicted on the victims are a mere reflection of a higher form of violence to which the demonstration testifies.'[64] In this sense, it can perhaps be said that violence in Sade serves only to *motivate the device*, as the Russian Formalists put it; it is necessary, but only in order to achieve the larger goal of revealing reason to be a form of violence. The implication of this claim, which is important for our purposes here, is that the presence of violence directed at others is not by itself sufficient to define sadism.

One must say the same for Masoch. Violence directed at the self is not sufficient to define masochism. Deleuze's analyses of Masoch suggest that actual physical violence is secondary in his works, just as they are in Sade's. This is evident, Deleuze suggests, in Masoch's use of language, which in contrast to Sade is educative not demonstrative. 'We are no longer in the presence of a torturer seizing upon a victim and enjoying her all the more because she is unconsenting and unpersuaded. We are dealing instead with a victim in search of a torturer.'[65] But the torturer must be made in the masochist's image of what a torturer should look like and their desire must be subordinated to the desire of the so-called victim. This is why the apparently sadistic characters in Masoch should not be confused with Sade's own creations; they are rather 'the realization of the masochistic fantasy' and quite different from anything that can be found in Sade. Wanda would be utterly out of place in Sade, just as Juliette would be utterly out of place in Masoch.[66] Moreover, the sadism exhibited by the apparently sadistic characters in Masoch is of a very different nature to Sade's libertines. For one thing, they need to be coerced into acting sadistically, and remain hesitant and doubtful throughout about their role, and even become resentful towards their victims, whereas Sade's characters act as they do instinctively and without hesitation or restraint. By the same token Sade's victims cannot be masochistic, not least because Sade's libertines would find that intolerable – their pleasure must be absolute! Masoch's language is dialectical, according to Deleuze; he works through transpositions and displacements – the tortured victim is in reality the master and the tormenting torturer is in reality the victim. It is this reasoning, which eroticizes dialectical reversals, that tantalizes and defines the masochist assemblage, not the accoutrements of the dungeon, much less the infliction of pain.

Sade and Masoch also differ at the level of ontology. Sade's work is underpinned by a twofold negation of both the negative as a partial process and what might be termed pure negation as an absolute. These two forms of negation correspond to the distinction between two natures in Sade elucidated by Klossowski. So-called secondary nature is 'pervaded by the negative' as Deleuze puts it, but since destruction 'is merely the reverse of creation and change' and 'disorder is another form of order' and so on, the negative processes it entails are necessarily partial.[67] This brings no joy to the sadist, indeed it is a cause of considerable disappointment, because it compromises the absolute form of pleasure he desires. He thus opposes secondary nature with a primary nature in which a pure form of negation reigns supreme, overriding the need to balance destruction and creation, disorder and order, and so on. 'Pure negation needs no foundation and is beyond all foundation, a primal delirium, an original and timeless chaos composed solely of wild and lacerating molecules.'[68] This pure form of negation corresponds to Freud's Death Instinct, which cannot be given in psychic life; as such, it is a delusion, but as Deleuze says, it is a delusion of reason itself, by which he means it is a delusion that arises out of the internal logic of Sade's thought. The pure evil the libertine is able to conjure in his mind as an Idea, as the product of his reason, is infinitely more potent to him than the sad and disappointing reality of what he can achieve in fact, as a matter of actual lived experience. That which cannot be experienced can only be demonstrated, hence the importance of language to Sade, and the need for repetition, which Deleuze suggests has an accelerating or intensifying effect. Multiplying both the victims and the monstrosities – which must consist of cruel actions as well as disgusting actions (as Pasolini's *Salò* only too vividly reminds us) – is Sade's way of trying, but ultimately failing, to leap from the realm of secondary nature to that of original nature.[69]

Masoch's work, by contrast, is defined by disavowal, which as Deleuze points out is in fact an entirely different operation to negation. It is 'an operation that consists neither in negating nor even destroying, but rather in radically contesting the validity of that which is: it suspends belief in and neutralizes the given in such a way that a new horizon opens up beyond the given and in place of it'.[70] Sade rejects the given, but Masoch doesn't; he simply turns his back on it and follows his own path, all the while carrying with him the knowledge that the neutralized real persists. He believes what he wants to believe, not what his eyes tell him he must believe, and his belief is a shield against what he doesn't want to think about. The clearest example of disavowal, according to Deleuze, is fetishism. The fetishized object is determined as the last object the child saw before becoming aware of castration, that is, before learning that women lack a penis. As such the fetish isn't a symbol; it is, rather, a frozen image, like a photograph, to which one returns helplessly, obsessively, to exorcize intrusive thoughts – unwelcome discoveries and such like – that threaten to disrupt one's status quo. The fetish is a point of departure, the beginning of a line of flight, representing the 'last point at which it was still possible to believe'.[71] Deleuze proposes that masochism needs to be understood in *temporal* terms. 'Formally speaking, masochism is a state of waiting; the masochist experiences waiting in its pure form'.[72] Pain is a necessary part of the masochist assemblage, to be sure, but it is not a source of pleasure. It is merely an effect.[73] 'The masochist waits for pleasure as something that is bound to be late, and expects pain as the condition that will finally ensure (both physically and morally) the advent of pleasure'.[74] Deleuze cautions us not to confuse the sequence of events, pain then pleasure, with causality.[75] Pain, he argues, only *'acquires significance in relation to the forms of repetition which condition its use'*.[76] Masochism, according to Deleuze, alters the 'normal' function of repetition in Freud's notion of the pleasure principle. Instead of repetition being governed by the idea of re-experiencing a previously experienced pleasure it *'runs wild* [déchaine] and becomes independent of all previous pleasure' and becomes an idea and ideal for itself.[77] Pleasure and repetition thereby exchange roles; pleasure now follows repetition and repetition precedes pleasure. Just as repetition is unchained from pleasure, so pleasure is unchained from repetition and similarly enabled to become a pure idea and ideal.

3

Territory

The key to understanding the concept of territory is chaos defined as an existential condition rather than a physical state of affairs (though it can be that too). This is ground zero for schizoanalysis. We see this very clearly in the chapter on the refrain in *A Thousand Plateaus*, which, despite its title, is really about the concept of territory. In a nice turn of phrase, Elizabeth Grosz defines the refrain as a 'kind of rhythmic regularity that brings a minimum of liveable order to a situation in which chaos beckons.'[1] Grosz does not expand on the phrase 'liveable order' herself, but in what follows I will try to expand upon it as a way of understanding territory. Territory is a liveable order produced and sustained by a refrain. For Deleuze and Guattari, chaos is an ever-present potentiality in both our mental lives and the physical world. All that we have, and all that we are, even the most stratified aspects of our lives, is nothing but a temporary victory over the relentless forces of chaos which are like a ground bass to our very existence. Deleuze and Guattari conceive chaos as both the absolute foundation for all thinking (it is the beginning and end of thought) and as a kind of relative dissolution of the senses and the sensible. It is, in other words, an ever-present possibility but one that is only realized in particular sets of circumstances. But it is never far away. It can never be entirely forgotten or ignored. Deleuze and Guattari speak of chaos threatening, stalking and trying to reabsorb the hard won sensibility of the concept.[2] But, even though they often speak of chaos as something to fear, and to ward off, they are equally adamant that without it, at least a bit of it, we would stultify and die. Chaos is both life and death. In *What is Philosophy?*, a book that is essentially organized around the notion of chaos, Deleuze and Guattari depict the disciplines of art, philosophy and science as being locked into an ageless battle against chaos. Each one fights chaos in its own way, but chaos is nevertheless the constant enemy. However, the aim of these battles is never to win completely, to shut out chaos altogether, because to do that would be to induce creative stasis – a form of death-in-life. The artist has to confront chaos and let it in and then try to give it form.

> Chaos is not an inert or stationary state, nor is it a chance mixture. Chaos makes chaotic and undoes every consistency in the infinite. The problem of philosophy [we could also say of life itself] is to acquire consistency without losing the infinite into which thought plunges (in this respect chaos has as much a mental as physical existence).[3]

There is, however, an art of dosages when it comes to chaos: one needs chaos, but only so much and not too much – just enough to disrupt 'normal service' so to speak and allow creativity to flow. As they often caution, one should not deterritorialize (i.e. allow chaos in) too quickly, and never completely; one needs to hold onto just enough territory to rebuild a life.[4] Deleuze and Guattari offer a vivid thumbnail sketch of this process in their account of the career of the great English painter J. W. Turner – his lifelong dance with chaos is depicted as courting breakdown in search of a breakthrough.[5] The danger of chaos is that it is attractive to us, under certain circumstances, and if we fall too deeply into it we may never escape it. This is why Deleuze and Guattari also refer to chaos as a black hole (it 'captures you and does not let you get out'[6]). Far from being a blank, undifferentiated morass, chaos has 'its own directional components, which are its own ecstasies.'[7] One sees this clearly in Artaud's work: 'I suffer hideously from life. There is no state I can attain. And it is certain that I have been dead for a long time, I have already committed suicide. ... I have no appetite for death, I have an appetite for not existing, for never having fallen into this interlude of imbecilities, abdications, renunciations, and obtuse encounters which is the self of Antonin Artaud, much weaker than he is. The self of this wandering invalid which from time to time presents its shadow on which he himself has spat, and long since, this crippled and shuffling self, this virtual, impossible self which nevertheless finds itself in reality. No one has felt its weakness as strongly as he, it is the principal, essential weakness of humanity. To destroy, to not exist.'[8] The temptation of the black hole is the temptation to opt out of life, to refuse to participate in its daily frustrations and inconsistencies, and instead plunge into a lightless world of disengagement.

The black hole does not pre-exist our actions, it is the product of our actions – it is, as Deleuze and Guattari put it, 'a machine effect in assemblages'.[9] Everything we do (insofar as it is an action of desire) carries this risk of plunging us into a black hole. In this sense then territory should be understood as a defensive concept because it describes our means of getting out of the black holes we sometimes find ourselves in either because we chose to go down a dark path or somehow our actions inadvertently lead us there. Deleuze and Guattari borrow F. Scott Fitzgerald's notion of the 'crack' from his short autobiographical piece *The Crack-up* to illustrate this idea. In life, according to Fitzgerald, there are three ways of cracking-up, that is, three ways the black hole can make itself felt in our daily lives. First, there are the big blows that hit you from the outside, that often present themselves in terms of choices – if only I hadn't drunk so much, if only I'd kept my mouth shut and so on. The changes that ensue, loss of love, loss of employment, loss of respect and so on, stay with you forever but also feel strangely alien because one feels that if one had made different choices things wouldn't be the way they are. Then there are the micro-cracks that occur when things seem to be going well – one might not even notice them at first. It is the corrosion that happens in one's soul when a thousand slights resonate together and ramify. The first time someone calls you 'fat' or 'loser' you might not even notice the hurt it caused, but the damage is done, and every repetition of that slight causes the hurt to magnify as it resonates within. Last, there are 'clean breaks'; these are the breaks you cannot come back from because it destroys all connection to the past. This is what people mean when they say about a former relationship that there is no 'us' anymore, there is nothing to go back to, the past has been volatized. We can also see that these are the types of situation that could drown us if we didn't have some kind of lifeline: territory is that lifeline.

In each case, the crack isn't to be found in the state of affairs, which may appear unchanged to the outside observer, despite the tumult within; the crack is in the territory which is our existential means of occupying the state of affairs, of making it liveable. 'Us' isn't a state of affairs, it is a territory that combines two or more worlds.[10] Our 'life' isn't a state of affairs either, it is an intermeshing of multiple territories. The cracks Fitzgerald speaks of are fissures in our most fundamental territory, namely our 'self', that allow too much darkness, too much chaos, to enter, and incapacitate 'us', temporarily or permanently. Deterritorialization, the process of leaving our territorial fortress, which defends against the despair of the potential black holes populating our existence, is thus highly dangerous, as Deleuze and Guattari frequently remind us. In its fullest sense, deterritorialization means functioning without territory, that is, freefalling into chaos without a safety net or harness, which is why whenever we deterritorialize we immediately seek opportunities to reterritorialize. So much so that we effectively only deterritorialize in order to reterritorialize, which is what happens when we change our minds or fall in love – we leave one territory so that we can immediately enter another. Deleuze and Guattari stipulate that there are three forms of deterritorialization, three ways of leaving our territory, or what they also call lines of flight (a line of flight is the path of a particular deterritorialization): (1) negative, (2) relative and (3) absolute. The negative deterritorialization is one that is overlaid by reterritorialization, which amounts to saying it is a form of change one undergoes in order to remain the same. The relative deterritorialization overcomes the inertia of reterritorialization, but can do so only in an ad hoc way, which means it never entirely escapes reterritorialization and sometimes ends up in a black hole all over again. Deterritorialization is absolute when it succeeds in creating a new earth, a new beginning, one that does not lead back to old territories – but just as this is the higher path, as it were, it is also the most dangerous because one form of absolute escape is death.[11]

> We cannot say that one of these three lines is bad and another good, by nature and necessarily. The study of the dangers of each line is the object of pragmatics or schizoanalysis, to the extent that it undertakes not to represent, interpret, or symbolize, but only to make maps and draw lines, marking their mixtures as well as their distinctions.[12]

Following Nietzsche and Castaneda, Deleuze and Guattari identify a variety of dangers associated with each species of line of flight. The shortlist of the most important dangers includes fear, clarity, power and disgust. We fear losing our security, all the comforts we have grown accustomed to, which define the very order of things ('the

binary machines that give us a well-defined status, the resonances we
enter into, the system of overcoding that dominates us – we desire all
that'[13]). We retreat in the face of the unknown and harden ourselves
against the call to change. We speak of the old days and call for a
return to the way things were – the fantasy of lost certainties. Clarity
is the feeling of knowing everything, of seeing through everything, of
being taken in by nothing. Instead of the great paranoias generated
by fear we have a multitude of microparanoias (which are every
bit as damaging), of seeing threats in even the smallest details: 'we
are trapped in a thousand little monomanias, self-evident truths,
and clarities that gush from every black hole and no longer form a
system, but are only rumble and buzz, blinding lights giving any and
everybody the mission of self-appointed judge, dispenser of justice,
policeman, neighbourhood SS man.'[14] Think here of the thousands of
people at Trump rallies shouting 'lock her up' or 'send them back', or
the people who voted in favour of Brexit because they saw Europe as
a mass of minor inconveniences and disagreeable regulations rather
than a grand project that ultimately benefited them. Power moves
between these two points of view (fear and clarity). 'Every man of
power jumps from one line to the other, alternating between a petty
and lofty style, the rogue's style and grandiloquent style, drugstore
demagoguery and the imperialism of the high-ranking government
man.'[15] He wants to stop the lines of flight that elude his control but
can only do so by creating a void. One thinks here of the awful 'spaces
of exception' (literally camps) created by politicians to contain asylum
seekers and refugees in a state of perpetual limbo rather than resettle
them. Agamben is surely right to see the proliferation of camps as one
the most damning indictments of our times.

The fourth danger, the great disgust, is in many ways the most
important. Here they invoke Fitzgerald again, specifically his famous
line that his 'self-immolation was something sodden-dark', as a

prelude to asking: 'Why is the line of flight a war one risks coming back from defeated, destroyed, after having destroyed everything one could?'[16] Why, in other words, does the attempt to escape from a black hole only increase the power of that black hole? Why instead of a way out does the line of flight turn out to be a way down? For Deleuze and Guattari it is only by recognizing the strange power of attraction of this particular line of flight, replete with its dangers, that we can understand fascism. 'Unlike the totalitarian State, which does its utmost to seal all possible lines of flight, fascism is constructed on an intense line of flight, which it transforms into a line of pure destruction and abolition.'[17] Fascism is suicidal rather than totalitarian, Deleuze and Guattari argue (following Virilio). 'Suicide is presented not as a punishment but as the crowning glory of the death of others.'[18] This is why the people cheered Hitler, they argue, because 'they wanted that death through the death of others.'[19] As they argued in *Anti-Oedipus*, there is no false consciousness or deception here: 'At a certain point, under a certain set of conditions, they wanted fascism, and it is the perversion of the desire of the masses that needs to be accounted for.'[20] The line of flight towards abolition and the black hole it terminates in should not be compared with or equated to the death drive. 'There are no internal drives in desire, only assemblages. Desire is always assembled; it is what the assemblage determines it to be. The assemblage that draws lines of flight is on the same level as they are, and is of the war machine type.'[21] In other words, what we call fascism is immanent to the assemblage, that is, it is generated by the assemblage, and not the unleashing of primeval instincts for violence and death. As such, it may be better to speak of the desire called fascism.[22]

The question at hand is how it is possible for the ordinary-seeming assemblages of everyday life such as prevailed in Germany in the 1930s could send an entire nation along the suicidal line of flight that precipitated the Second World War and all the ensuing horrors. Unfortunately they only hint at an answer to the question, but their speculation (also borrowed from Virilio) is that the manifold miseries of daily life (clarity) snowball into a longing for a 'clean break'. Exit polls following both Brexit and Trump's election pointed to exactly this type of desire: people wanted change, they wanted disruption for a million different reasons, and so they voted for the disruptors, regardless of whether they believed it would be a change for the better. Many commentators have speculated whether this turn of events constitutes the appearance of a new stage of fascism. Whether or not Trump, in particular, is a fascist is the subject of considerable debate among leftist commentators without anyone being able to decide one way or another. In large part this is because the historical comparisons don't really stack up. Trump's regime has neither been as murderous as Hitler's nor as ideologically uniting. Hitler's popularity at the start of his reign greatly exceeds Trump's, even among his most ardent supporters. And Hitler was also obviously in favour of war which Trump, to his credit, does not seem to be. Indeed in his early campaigning in 2015 he spoke against America's invasion of Iraq and Afghanistan, describing it as self-defeating. Umberto Eco's proposition that every age has its own fascism, which Lawrence Grossberg cites approvingly, is I think very useful here because it sets aside the tedious problem of historical comparison and allows us to focus instead on the new ways in which the love of power manifests itself. But in contrast to Grossberg, who argues that American fascism is 'defined by its reconfiguration of the nation state', I want to suggest instead that it is defined in terms of the particularity of its line of flight towards death.[23]

One could point to a variety of examples to evidence this, but the starkest illustration of this line of flight I've seen (precisely because it is so banal and benign seeming) is Disney's appropriation and transformation of *Star Wars* characters into theme park attractions. A couple of days before Donald Trump was inaugurated as the forty-fifth president of the United States of America, I took my kids to that most American of places, Walt Disney World in Orlando. This was in early 2017, five years after Disney purchased Lucasfilm and two years before the dedicated *Star Wars* section of the park Galaxy's Edge opened. There were a couple of makeshift *Star Wars*-themed areas and rides open at this stage. However, every hour or so, the familiar 'da, da, da, da, da-da' refrain of the Emperor's march would suddenly blast from loudspeakers all over the park and a platoon of storm troopers led by Captain Phasma would assemble in the main square and then proceed to march in formation down Main Street USA. I remember being surprised by this because intuitively one would expect to see the 'good guys', that is, the rebels, marching and not the 'bad guys'. And yet at every turn we were far more likely to see representatives of the dark side, from the ubiquitous storm troopers to Darth Vader and Kylo Ren, than the heroes of the good side, such as Luke Skywalker or Princess Leia. This was true even in the many merchandise outlets, where Darth Vader and the storm troopers were easily the most frequently represented characters on T-shirts, coffee mugs and backpacks. As surprised as I was to see the prominence given to storm troopers and Darth Vader in the happiest place on earth, the more I thought about it the more fitting it seemed. Maybe it was because the Trump inauguration was only days away, but I couldn't help but think that in a country like the United States, which is many ways the most powerful imperial nation in history, it is apt that the dark side of the force should be attractive to so many people (and not just to Americans, I hasten to add, since millions of overseas tourists like myself also visit Disney theme parks).

It appeared to me to be living proof that black holes do indeed have their own directional components, which are its ecstasies.

It is not the ecstasy of some vague evil, however. The appeal is, I think, quite specific. The appeal of storm troopers is the appeal of planet destroyers. It is doubtless no accident that the central plot of every *Star Wars* movie has been to save entire planets from literal obliteration. The death star in all its incarnations is the ultimate black hole – it not only brings death, it invites us to marvel at its power, to feel its libidinal tractor beam, and recognize it as the embodiment of everything that we fear and desire: death as life. The environment has always paid the price of human advancement, but it is only in the last few decades that humanity has become collectively conscious of the fact that our actions are pushing the planet in a direction that will no longer support life as we know it. To continue to profit from the destruction of the planet and to facilitate that destruction as Trump is doing by rolling back legislation designed to protect what remains can only be called environmental profiteering. As is the case with war profiteering, environmental profiteering takes advantage of a crisis for the sake of making money and resists all efforts to end the crisis because that would put an end to its profits. This is our situation now. The technology exists to switch most of our energy needs to renewable sources, but governments and corporations everywhere resist this because it would spell the end of a multi-billion dollar industry. Therefore the strange attraction Trump exerts on a small, but sufficient percentage of American voters is literally a line of abolition because the failure to arrest global warming will jeopardize the lives of all living creatures on earth, not just humans. The fact that multi-billionaires like Amazon's CEO Jeff Bezos are fantasizing about colonizing Mars (as Rhodes once did) is of a piece with this line of abolition because it embraces and actively seeks to profit from the end of the world as we know it.

We territorialize because we need to and we need to territorialize because we have to confront chaos, both in its originary form and in the form of black holes. The territory transforms not only the elements constituting it but its inhabitant as well (as both the territory's creator and primary beneficiary). We not only act differently in our territory from the way we act outside it but we effectively are different and derive a specific surplus value from being this way – for example, the feeling of 'comfort' we experience in our home is a surplus value of the specific kind of territory we call 'home', and not merely an affordance derived from the material circumstances of our accommodation. I do not mean to deny the importance of affordance, a concept that is lately very fashionable indeed, but I do insist that it is a secondary consideration. We have to be wary of turning affordances into efficient causes. We adapt our sense of homeliness to fit our circumstances and not the other way around, which is why a hovel can be homely and a mansion unhomely. It is also why words like 'saudade' exist: there is no more keenly felt lack than the exile's feeling of lacking a home. To feel 'at home' is not the same thing as being 'at home' and the difference between the two is not simply a matter of affect. The territory is composed of elements it borrows or steals from the environment we find ourselves in (our milieu) and organizes into new worlds. These elements are signs, or even more basically perceptual stimuli, which can of course take a number of different forms, from visual displays of plumage, to odours, to songs, and even elaborate physical constructions such as the stagemaker bird's stage made of twigs and upturned leaves.[24] The elements by themselves do not constitute the territory; they have to be arranged with what we might usefully describe as territorial intent. Doubtless this word 'intent' will trouble many, but it is clear from the examples Deleuze and Guattari work through that territory is not happenstance, it is produced quite deliberately with a precise set of effects in mind.

This does not mean, however, that territories are optional, or incidental to our lives. On the contrary, as Deleuze and Guattari conceive it, territory is not something we can do without – our whole lives are spent building, enlarging, escaping, remodelling or leaving our territories. Life is a constant, ongoing process of territorializing. As such, it should be clear by now that territory is neither a spatial concept nor a material concept. This does not mean that it does not entail either spatial or material components, I hasten to add, but it is to say that in Deleuze and Guattari's work these aspects of the concept of territory are not considered primary. Counter-intuitively, Deleuze and Guattari argue that material components are not used to create a territory, rather it is the territorializing process (the T-factor as Deleuze and Guattari put it) which transforms materials into signs and thereby paves the way to the production of territory. Similarly, the space of the territory cannot easily be mapped or correlated with the proverbial 'facts on the ground'. In many cases the territory has no specific spatial dimension, it is all 'in our heads', and it is better understood as a feeling, or better yet a sense of purpose. Rather than regard them as spaces, it would be more useful and accurate to see territories as subjective states in a psychological sense, which is how the ethologist Jakob von Uexküll, one of the key theorists from whom Deleuze and Guattari lifted the concept of territory, suggests we should see them.[25] He writes, 'Territory is purely a problem of the environment because it represents an exclusively subjective product, the presence of which even the most detailed knowledge of the surroundings offers no explanation at all.'[26] We can literally hum or whistle them into being, no matter what our actual circumstances are.

In spite of their frequent recourse to the work of animal behaviour studies theorists (e.g. Lorenz, Tinbergen and Uexküll), and their terminology, Deleuze and Guattari do not simply lift the concept of territory from ethology and apply it tout court to the analysis of the everyday lives of humans. Nor do they propose, as Lorenz did, that animal behaviour (broadly understood) can be used to explain human behaviour, as though all species were somehow the same at a deep instinctual level. In fact, they vigorously dispute ethology's construction of the concept of territory in terms of aggression (Lorenz) precisely because it would make aggression 'the phylogenetic evolution of an instinct' and offer their own version of it as a corrective.[27] In fact, the inspiration for the concept of territory seems not to have been animal-related at all, rather it appears to have been clinical, as the following passage from the refrain chapter in *A Thousand Plateaus* would seem to suggest: 'Two schizophrenics converse or stroll according to laws of boundary and territory that may escape us.'[28] It is apparent from the behaviour of schizophrenics – but not only schizophrenics – that the basic tenets of behaviouralism are too narrowly conceived to account for the abundant variety of ways of being in the world that are evident all around us. One cannot fully fathom the logic of the schizophrenics' territory merely by observing them; one must also know what they are thinking, and how they are seeing the world. Deleuze and Guattari move away from physiological models of behaviour premised on some variety of stimulus and response and its cognates such as inhibition and release, and replace them with productive desire understood as an assemblage-making process, precisely because those models cannot cope with what we might think of as the imaginative and symbolic dimensions of everyday life. Their basic complaint against standard behaviouralist ways of thinking is that it is too linear because it follows a kind of billiard-ball logic of causality, whereas their model is compositional.[29] The territory is an art work, or better yet an art event.[30]

For Deleuze and Guattari, territory is essentially a pragmatic concept (ethology, in their view, would be better served if it paid more attention to pragmatics). As I have already indicated, territory has a clinical meaning in Deleuze and Guattari's work as well; they use it

to explain how we manage intersubjectivity, particularly the feelings
of anxiety this can occasion. The link between these two conceptions
of territory (pragmatic and clinical) is the *refrain* understood as a
performative (in J. L. Austin's sense of the word) and not just as a little
ditty one plays or sings, that is, it is that which brings the territory
into being by power of its performance. When we whistle to ourselves
to allay our anxiety or just announce to the world that we are happy
we are performing a self-transforming act, which is at once pragmatic
and psychological in its effect. Our whistling has purpose as well as
meaning. 'A child hums to summon the strength for the schoolwork
she has to hand in. A housewife sings to herself, or listens to the radio,
as she marshals the antichaos forces of her work. ... For sublime
deeds like the foundation of a city or the fabrication of a golem, one
draws a circle, or better yet walks in a circle as in a children's dance,
combining rhythmic vowels and consonants that correspond to the
interior forces of creation.'[31] In sum, territory is an *act*, a *passage*, not
a space.[32] It is the composition of one's own world.

Territorializing is world-making (black holes are the unmaking of
worlds). It is in this sense that it is appropriately understood as a form
of pragmatics. Deleuze and Guattari's version of pragmatics, a word
they use interchangeably with schizoanalysis as the global name for
their methodology, is drawn from Austin's theory of performativity,
as I mentioned, but it also incorporates the insights of Deleuze and
Guattari's contemporaries Benveniste and Ducrot. However, Deleuze
and Guattari take the theory of performativity much further than
any of these scholars did – outside the narrow confines of pure
linguistics and into the varied realms of everyday life. Austin saw
the performative as a peculiar part of speech which no one else until
then had noticed or written about. He was interested in it because it
is a form of language that literally accomplishes something outside
of itself, and indeed outside of the usual jurisdictions of linguistic

concern such as the production of meaning and sense-making. The expressed of a performative is an action rather than a meaning. For example, when a judge passes sentence on someone at a trial their words do much more than make meaning, they bring about an actual change in the circumstances of the convicted subject, which is then no longer a matter for linguistics but instead belongs to the domain of a new discipline Deleuze and Guattari call pragmatics. Austin did not take this step himself, but it is the inevitable next step as Deleuze and Guattari and several other commentators have observed. 'As long as linguistics confines itself to constants, whether syntactical, morphological, or phonological, it ties the statement to a signifier and enunciation to a subject and accordingly botches the assemblage. ... As Vološinov [Bakhtin] says, so long as linguistics extracts constants, it is incapable of helping us understand how a single word can be a complete enunciation.'[33] There has to be something else that is beyond linguistics but not beyond language that can explain this. 'The order-word [i.e. the performative] is precisely that variable that makes the word as such an enunciation.'[34]

Deleuze and Guattari describe the process initiated by the performative as an incorporeal transformation because – to continue with the same example – the corporeal body of the convicted remains the same, but it takes on new (social) attributes which change the way that person can interact in society.[35] Although Deleuze and Guattari are often portrayed as theorists of the body, they were actually more interested in the way the non-bodily, that is, words, can transform the body, without ever penetrating beneath the surface. For Deleuze and Guattari, it is the instantaneous nature of the transformation (which they suggest can be projected back to the origin of society), which is of uppermost importance – it is the reason all the plateaus are precisely dated.[36] This line of thinking can be traced back to Deleuze's discussion of the Stoics in *The Logic of Sense*. The Stoics were the first to theorize the form of content and the form of expression as autonomous but interacting functions. 'The form of expression is constituted by the warp of expresseds, and the form of content by the woof of bodies.'[37] When a knife cuts flesh, or someone climbs a mountain, there is an intermingling of bodies – knives, flesh, mountains – but the statements 'the knife is cutting flesh' and 'Mallory attempted to climb Everest' express incorporeal transformations of a very different order, which are nonetheless attributed to bodies. 'In expressing the noncorporeal attribute, and by that token attributing it to the body, one is not representing or referring but *intervening* in a way; it is a speech act.'[38] That is the uncanny power of the performative. Austin always treated the performative as a part of speech and never ceased to think of language as primary, but Deleuze and Guattari reject this for not being abstract enough. In their view, the performative *is the condition of possibility of language itself.*[39] Performatives disclose the fact that the outside of language – not merely the circumstances in which language is used but the social acts language accomplishes – is always already immanent to language.

Performing acts with and through language is not simply one of the things we can do with language, it is why we have language. 'The only possible definition of language', according to Deleuze and Guattari, 'is the set of all order-words, implicit presuppositions, or speech acts current in a language at a given moment.'[40] Doubtless this claim seems a little extreme, but that is to misunderstand the deeper point Deleuze and Guattari are trying to make, which is to overturn the widespread assumption in structuralist linguistics (which was dominant in France in the 1970s when they were writing *A Thousand Plateaus*) that language is a universal in its own right, capable of being explained and understood in the absence of non-linguistic enabling conditions.[41] They acknowledge that it is difficult to assign language a non-linguistic starting point but argue that this is because language is not inherently representational. It does not move between something seen or felt and something said but rather flows from one saying to another saying.[42] 'Language is not content to go from a first party to a second party, from one who has seen to one who has not, but necessarily goes from a second party to a third party, neither of whom has seen. It is in this sense that language is the transmission of the word as order-word, not the communication of a sign as information.'[43] But it is not speaking subjects who issue the orders that language transmits, it is language itself (providing we understand that language is not primary, the order-word is), or what Deleuze and Guattari refer to as the *collective assemblage of enunciation*. 'There is no individual enunciation. There is not even a subject of enunciation. Yet relatively few linguists have analysed the necessarily social character of enunciation.'[44] This becomes clear, they argue, when we examine how free indirect discourse functions in literature.

Even when the usual markers of who said this and thought that are absent and we are not told whether it is thoughts, dreams, fantasies or words spoken silently in someone's head, we can nonetheless make sense of what we read because the underpinning assemblage makes the distribution of subjects and statements clear. What we call direct discourse is extracted from indirect discourse, not the other way around.[45] Deleuze and Guattari argue that this is true of all language use. The 'statement is individuated, and enunciation subjectified, only to the extent that an impersonal collective assemblage requires it and determines it to be so.'[46] It is in this sense that '*I* is an order-word.'[47] When we say 'I' we extract a self, a proper name and even a cogito, from the constellation of voices that constitutes the collective assemblage of enunciation. But we could not say 'I' if the position 'I' did not exist in our society as the expressed of the statement 'I am'. We take it for granted that the

'I' is the starting point for all thinking about the nature of society but that assumes what must in fact be explained. This is why, too, Deleuze and Guattari always say writing (particularly literature) takes place at the level of the real, and not the imaginary or the symbolic. They are not saying the performative is therefore the origin of language (it is merely a language-function in their eyes); nor are they saying the explicit order or direct command is the only form the performative can take (they are merely the most common variants of the performative). In fact, the performative in its guise as order-word is to be found everywhere in language where an act is linked to the expressed of a statement by power of social obligation. And, according to Deleuze and Guattari, every statement displays this link, including that most foundational of statements 'I am'.[48]

The expressed of an expression is not its meaning; it is the *transformation* of the world the expression instantiates. When the judge says 'you are guilty' to someone, the effect on that person is not merely semantic, from that moment on they literally are no longer free, they are convicts, and they are tarnished with all the associations our society makes with that state of being. Their whole world is changed and so is ours because their place in it has been altered. The expressed of the statement 'you are guilty' is the transformation of subject of that statement – the 'you' – who is instantly re-positioned in society as being on the 'wrong side of the law'. To be sure, not everyone who utters this phrase will be able to induce this effect – only properly authorized people can do it – but that does not alter the fact that at an abstract level the expressed of an expression is always a transformation of the subject of the expressed. Moreover, that authorization is itself the expressed of several interconnecting statements – you have a law degree, you are appointed judge, you are empowered to decide this case and so on. Underpinning this state of affairs is the material fact that this is a society in which there are such things as laws, judges and convicts and is organized in such a way that statements of the 'you are guilty' variety are not merely possible but are in a certain sense redundant because we take it for granted that a person's place in society can and should be distributed according to their relative position in relation to an abstract ideal of guilty or not guilty.

The example of the judge passing sentence highlights the rarely acknowledged dualism at the heart of assemblage theory. 'If in a social field we distinguish the set of corporeal modifications and the set of incorporeal transformations, we are presented, despite the variety in each of the sets, with two formalizations, one of content, the other of expression. ... Precisely because content, like expression, has a form of its own, one can never assign the form of expression the function of simply representing, describing, or averring a corresponding content: there is neither correspondence nor conformity.'[49] We can think of this as the relationship between two kinds of event, the ongoing and essentially linear process of the time of the body, which we think of as 'aging', unfolding according to a regular schedule and enacting gradual modification, and the sharp, instantaneous interventions and disruptions of incorporeal categories like the 'age of majority'. Your body may not feel any different the day before and the day after you turn eighteen, but its situation has been completely changed, it has passed from childhood into adulthood, all without changing anything in a physical or physiological sense. The assemblage theorizes the possibility of this juncture between these two temporalities. In other words, the assemblage is neither the prisoner's body (content) nor the judge's sentence (expression), nor even their combination: rather it is the set of conditions that enable someone to lose their freedom, perhaps their life, because of the say so of another person. The assemblage takes the form of a reciprocal presupposition between two formalizations – content and expression – brought together by power of the intervention of a form of expression into a form of content in answer to a destabilization or problematization of the social field. This way of thinking, which owes a great deal to Foucault's work, can be seen clearly in Foucault's histories, especially his work on madness, which charts the different ways madness has been produced as a 'problem', which has in turn led to the generation of a vast discourse about madness (expression) as well as the various forms of confinement of people designated as mad (content). In contrast to Foucault, Deleuze and Guattari are not specifically concerned with either expression or content; they are interested rather in the articulation of the two. This articulation mechanism is the assemblage.

Territories appear where they are required and the T-factor is mobilized. The T-factor is not an emergent property, as many versions of assemblage theory seem to think; it is not something that spontaneously 'just happens' when certain materials come together; rather it is an intrinsic capacity of the assemblage, or better yet, it is one of the reasons why assemblages exist. Territorializing is necessary to our existence as social beings. 'The territory is first of all the critical distance between two beings of the same species: Mark your distance. What is mine is first of all my distance; I possess only distances. Don't anybody touch me, I growl if anyone enters my territory. Critical distance is a relation based on matters of expression. It is a question of keeping at a distance the forces of chaos knocking at the door.'[50] When chaos threatens, we create a territory using the resources we have to hand. 'If need be, I'll put my territory on my own body, I'll territorialize my body: the house of the tortoise, the hermitage of the crab, but also tattoos that make the body a territory.'[51] Critical distance is the minimum amount of separation two creatures of the same species require in order to coexist in proximity to one another. Harold Garfinkel's breach experiments offer a vivid illustration of this point.

For example, in one experiment he asked his students to ride elevators in office buildings and stand as close as possible to the other people in the car and record their reactions. In crowded elevators people barely noticed, but in empty elevators it was seen as an encroachment and generally provoked negative reactions from unsuspecting test subjects. As this example illustrates, territory has two key functions: it regulates the coexistences of subjects by defining how much space they need for their comfort and security and it maximizes the number of co-inhabitants of a particular space by assigning them 'specialist' roles. This in turn has two key effects: the reorganization of functions and the regrouping of forces.[52]

In social terms, these two territorial effects are registered in the formation of occupations and trades (reorganization of functions) and the founding of belief systems (regrouping of forces). In doing so the territory, or rather territorializing, 'unleashes something that will surpass it'.[53] The territory transforms forces of chaos into forces of the earth – the territory is the 'new earth' Deleuze and Guattari often speak of. It is not merely the ground beneath our feet but an intense centre, a 'natal' where we feel 'at home'. In this moment, when the *territory comes into being* the milieu components cease to be *directional* (i.e. functional) and instead become *dimensional* (i.e. expressive).[54] The key difference between functional and expressive signs is this: the latter cannot be reduced to or thought of as the 'effects of an impulse triggering an action in a milieu'.[55] Expressive signs are 'auto-objective', which means they 'find an objectivity in the territory they draw'.[56] This means they change the dynamic of the interaction between the signal emitter and their circumstances from a mechanistic stimulus-response scenario (or what Deleuze would later call in his books on cinema the sensory-motor scheme) to a more complex interior-exterior scenario (or what Deleuze later called the time-image). The boundary the territory constructs is not spatial – though it may take a spatial form – but subjective: the territory is the 'space' in which my interiority (i.e. 'my' subjectivity as 'I' experience it) can be experienced as my 'home' and everything that is not 'homely' to me is confined to the exteriority of what we refer to as our circumstances. The crucial point is that, as Deleuze's analysis of the birth of the time-image in cinema pointed out, the circumstances cannot be called upon to explain the meaning of the signs.

> In *Umberto D*, De Sica constructs the famous sequence quoted as an example by Bazin: the young maid going into the kitchen in the morning, making a series of mechanical, weary gestures, cleaning a bit, driving the ants away from a water fountain, picking up the coffee grinder, stretching out her foot to close the door with her toe. And her eyes meet her pregnant woman's belly, and it is as though all the misery in the world were going to be born ... what has suddenly been brought about is a pure optical situation to which the little maid has no response or reaction.[57]

Deleuze goes onto enumerate several other examples in which this same kind of sequence is played out – *Germany Year 0*, *Stromboli*, *Europe 51* and *The Lonely Woman* – in each case what is decisive is the emergence of a new type of image, one that is 'fundamentally distinct from the sensory-motor situations of the action-image in the old realism'. Characters no longer react to their situations. The action on screen is instead driven by something that rises from within them. Deleuze regards this moment in cinema as pivotal because it not only launched a new style of film (i.e. neo-realism), it also changed the very nature of cinematic narration by opening up a new possibility for the motivation of action. It can also be seen as the moment when cinema became conscious of territory because it marks a clear line of distinction between the unseen interiority of characters and the equally unseen exterior relations that obtain between them and their circumstances. 'For this relation can be given without the circumstances being given, just as the relation to the impulses can be given without the impulse being given. And even when the impulses and circumstances are given, the relation is prior to what it places in relation. Relations between matters of expression express relations of the territory to internal impulses and external circumstances: they have an autonomy within this very expression.'[58] In the territory, the signs relate to each other, thus creating what we might call – borrowing from Arnold van Gennep and Victor Turner – a 'liminal space' because it is a space produced by the deliberate mobilization of signs and more especially because it is a space of transition. To the outside observer the placement of these signs often appears ritualistic, but they are better understood as territorializing because they induce the equivalent of a new species.[59] The liminal space is a space of transition (not just a kind of in-between or limbo space as it is often characterized, which refers only to the middle phase of the 'rite of passage'); in the primitive societies Turner studies, for example, it is the place of transition for young people from childhood to adulthood.[60] This is the essential power of territory; it not only creates a home for the subject, sheltering them from chaos, it can also induce sufficient differentiation in the subject such that it induces the production of a new subject.[61]

Returning to cinema, territory is found in the film's quirks, the moments when directional signs become dimensional in other words. What that looks like in practice will vary from case to case. Let me offer one quick illustration, Denzel Washington's character Robert McCall in *The Equalizer* movies directed by Antoine Fuqua (2014, 2018). He has a very specific 'skill set' (to use Hollywood's favourite euphemism for military training) which define him as an action figure in the same mould as characters played by Clint Eastwood (*Dirty Harry*), Liam Neeson (*Taken*), Tom Cruise (*Mission Impossible, Jack Reacher*), Bruce

Willis (*Die Hard*), Matt Damon (*Bourne*) and Keanu Reeves (*John Wick*). He has an uncanny ability to kill the 'enemy' using any available weapon – the more unlikely the weapon the better, for example, the infamous pencil in *John Wick* – and an equally uncanny (some would say improbable) ability to survive even the most brutalizing assaults, falls, bullet wounds, stabbings and so on. His character is 'rounded out' as it were by a similarly familiar set of personality traits shared by all the aforementioned 'heroes' such as the de rigueur unassuming and mild manner masking profound self-confidence (i.e. the absolute certainty they will prevail regardless of the odds), the laconic jokes at the expense of the victim, the eye-for-an-eye sense of justice, the impassivity when dealing out rough justice and so on. All of these are expected and we may say all are intended to trigger a fairly predictable range and variety of affects including, but not limited to, affection for the hero, sympathy for his situation (which is always depicted as unjust), concern for his continued well-being, and a visceral thrill when he triumphs over impossible odds and vanquishes all and restores justice.

All of these traits are directional. They point to a very specific type of character and very specific set of affects, both of which audiences the world over have learned to recognize and depending on their tastes appreciate. They have become bankable characteristics from the movie studio's point of view, so one doesn't see or expect much variation on this basic pattern, which is obviously a problem because just as audiences enjoy familiarity, they also get bored with artless repetition. And so these characters are also endowed with peculiar foibles (their signature) that set them apart from each other and give them a distinctive *style*, which takes us from the realm of milieu to that of territory. Style is dimensional not directional for Deleuze and Guattari, therefore it is not to be found in the familiar clutch of character traits that are calculated to reliably produce the set of affects we associate with action heroes today. We have to look elsewhere, as Deleuze and Guattari do, which explains their fascination with non-mainstream (in the context of French philosophy) authors like Artaud, Burroughs, Beckett, Kafka and Kerouac. In the case of the character Robert McCall we do not have to look too far to find mannerisms that are clearly not part of the same ensemble of traits that signify his hero status. They are similarly conspicuous, but neither their meaning nor purpose is immediately obvious. Deleuze makes explicit the connection between style and assemblage in his extended conversation with Claire Parnet in *Dialogues*:

> I should like to say what a style is. It belongs to people of whom you normally say, 'They have no style.' This is not a signifying structure, nor a reflected organization, nor a spontaneous inspiration, nor an orchestration, nor a little piece of music. It is an assemblage, an assemblage of enunciation. A style is managing to stammer in one's own language. It is difficult, because there has to be a need for such stammering. Not being a stammerer in one's speech, but being a stammerer of language itself. Being like a foreigner in one's own language. Constructing a line of flight.[62]

He goes on to say,

> Life is like that too. In life there is a sort of awkwardness, a delicacy of health, a frailty of constitution, a vital stammering which is someone's charm. Charm is the source of life just as style is the source of writing. Life is not your history – those who have no charm have no life, it is as though they are dead. But the charm is not the person. It is what makes people be grasped as so many combinations and so many unique chances from which such a combination has been drawn.[63]

To begin with, there is his reading list. He doesn't simply read books, which is unusual enough for an action hero; he conscientiously works

his way through a list of 100 books one is supposed to read before
one dies. We could see it as signifying (directional sign) that he is an
intellectual, and not just a thug and a killer, that he is old-fashioned
and therefore attached to an older purer form of justice, that he is
sensitive and worldly, and none of these readings would be wrong.
But one cannot but feel that there is more to it than that. His reading
list is presented as his way of working through his grief over his wife's
untimely death, but it also betrays an OCD tendency that sends the
character down a different kind of line of flight, one that is no longer
tied to his 'hero's journey' (dimensional sign). This is made manifest
in at least three other sequences in the film that patently play no part
in driving the narrative forwards and could therefore be considered
otiose. These are largely but not exclusively centred on his eating
rituals. First, there is the careful setting out of his spotlessly clean
white napkin and cutlery before eating or even making a cup of tea;
then there is the diligent polishing and setting out and display of green
apples; and last, there is the seemingly compulsive need to immediately
wash up after eating. I suppose one could read this as a sign that he
doesn't like to leave a trace of his presence, but then he doesn't wear
gloves or worry about fingerprints or other tell-tale evidence, so I don't
think this holds. Undoubtedly his most peculiar quirk is his habit of
using his stopwatch to time his violent encounters. All of these traits
could be considered directional in the sense that they depict him as
eccentric and slightly odd thus eliciting sympathy, but they do more
than that too, they create what Deleuze and Guattari call an auto-
objectivity. They give the character 'a life' (in Deleuze's sense) that
rises above and goes beyond the machinic traits of vengeful killer,
which is what the plot demands, and in doing so create a territory
that we as an audience can occupy.

Style is, in this sense, an exercise in redundancy – the more
distinctive it is, the greater its power of redundancy, meaning the

more we are able to internalize it and know its inner rhythms. One has only to think of one's favourite style of music, whether that is rock, jazz, classical or tango to know this in a visceral way. The tapping foot, the thrumming fingers, the swinging hips, are the body's way of knowing music, but it is also evidence of redundancy. Redundancy does not inhibit, much less negate creativity, on the contrary it demands it – the rules of the game do not determine how the game will be played, only how it can be played. As any jazz enthusiast can attest, the spectrum of music that counts as jazz is as diverse as it is contested. But even as the canon of jazz standards has grown, no one can accuse it of lacking in creativity.

4

Expressive Materialism

Assemblage theory, more so than most theories it sometimes seems, is subject to several misconceptions, which weigh it down and prevent it from being developed into a method.[1] One of the most pernicious of these misconceptions, as I noted in the Introduction, is the tendency to treat the assemblage as a physical entity cobbled together from random bits of material like a potluck dinner or a patchwork quilt. The most sophisticated iteration of this additive model of the assemblage (as I call it) is Jane Bennett's well-known and widely endorsed definition of assemblages as 'ad hoc groupings of diverse elements of vibrant materials of all sorts.'[2] There is a common sense quality to the idea that the assemblage is something assembled from miscellaneous things that is difficult to argue with because the very word 'assemblage' seems to be saying precisely and completely obviously *that* (yet another reason why it might be best if we stopped using the word 'assemblage' altogether and reverted to the original French word 'agencement'). The very fact that it seems like common sense that the assemblage is something *assembled* from miscellaneous things should be enough to make us suspicious because if that's all it is saying then it is saying very little. If, as Bennett argues, assemblages are just ad hoc groupings it is difficult to see the utility of the concept, save that it names randomly formed heterogeneous entities. It is hard to escape this conclusion because Bennett insists again and again that whatever agency or power

– capacity, capability and so on – the assemblage might have only emerges out of the interaction between its randomly thrown together elements. Under these conditions it can have neither intention nor purpose, which as I argue in what follows creates several problems that cannot be solved within the terms Bennett sets for herself.

Bennett's model of the assemblage is like a souffle that has failed to rise and it is our job to ask why it falls flat, to see what ingredients are missing in its formulation, and use that knowledge to deepen our understanding of Deleuze and Guattari's version of the concept. My contention is that it falls flat because she tries to see it as an entity, albeit a processual entity, whereas for Deleuze and Guattari it is a dynamic arrangement between two (or more) semi-autonomous formations that encompasses the organization of bodies and the organization of discourses. Bennett's project is to use the notion of the assemblage to show the 'limitations in human-centred theories of action'[3] and demonstrate the extent to which contemporary society is populated by institutions and systems that bridge the human and non-human divide. This is clearly one implication of Deleuze and Guattari's work, for example, the man-horse assemblage they associate with the war-machine, but Bennett's mobilization of it is at odds with their project. Putting it in the starkest of terms, her work constantly seeks to diminsh the responsibility of humans (not just individual humans but humanity itself) for the circumstances we find ourselves in. She does this by first of all reducing humans to the status of bit players in the theatre of life, which includes a huge cast of characters – actants – of varying scales from electrons and microbes up to corporations and governments; she then defines agency as a power that emerges as a result of the interactions between all the cast members. Individual cast members retain their capacity to disrupt the performance, or even strike off on their own to start something else, but the power of the assemblage as a whole owes entirely to their interactions.

'An assemblage owes its agentic capacity to the vitality of the materials that constitute it.' She goes onto suggest this vitality is comparable to the Chinese notion of *shi*, which she defines as 'vibratory', an 'élan inherent to a specific arrangement of things.'[4] As can be seen, her model of the assemblage, in complete contrast to Deleuze and Guattari's, makes no place for the specificities of human desire. Deleuze and Guattari explicitly rule out the idea that desire can or should be thought of as an undifferentiated energy. But even more importantly, Bennett's formulation is all substance and no form – Bennett does not show any interest in the form taken by assemblages, it is almost as if for her that is irrelevant; all that matters is the vibratory energy of the substances trapped in the net of a particular assemblage. For Bennett *shi* emmanates from the assemblage; it is produced by and projected out of the assemblage as the product of its combined elements. 'A coffee house or school house is a mobile configuration of people, insects, odors, ink, electrical flows, air currents, caffeine, tables, chairs, fluids, and sounds. Their *shi* might at one time consist in the mild and ephemeral effluence of good vibes, and at another in a more dramatic force capable of engendering a philosophical movement or political movement, as it did in the café's of Jean-Paul Sartre's and Simone de Beauvoir's Paris and in the Islamist schools in Pakistan in the late twentieth century.'[5] This is an astonishing claim. Can one really credit Paris's cafés with the invention of existentialism? Did not certain beer halls in Germany also play a part? Not to mention the trains Sartre and others took to get to Germany and back. However, if we grant that the premise of this thesis is plausible, and I have to admit to being skeptical that it is, it actually leaves us none the wiser as to how existentialism came into being, save that it was the product of some unfathomable alchemy involving people, insects, odours, ink, electrical flows, air currents, caffeine, tables, chairs, fluids and sounds.

If existentialism is the product of the interactions of all these material things then how did it come into being? How were these elements selected? What power of selection was in operation? What brought these elements together? How did they interact? What caused them to interact in the way they did? Moreover, how did these material things – people, insects, odours, ink, electrical flows, air currents, caffeine, tables, chairs, fluids and sounds – combine to give rise to an essentially discursive or expressive entity like existentialism? How did the material capture the immaterial? Bennett doesn't address any of these questions. Indeed she makes no place for questions of this type because in her model the assemblage is ad hoc and almost exclusively material. (She tends to treat nonmaterial discursive or expressive forms as though they were materials.) Ultimately, what Bennett offers isn't so much an explanation of the rise of existentialism in Paris as a highly original starting point for an inquiry, one that takes more seriously than is customarily the case the actual environment in which exisentialism arose. Admittedly it is an exciting starting point, one whose scope has been widened considerably beyond the traditional boundaries for such history of thought inquiries to include that which is usually excluded, but it lacks any way of explaining how and why these particular materials came together in the way they did. There is no theory of their organizational structure either. And the only explanation offered for the fact their combination has any effect is that the materials are intrinsically vibratory.

There is a strong writerly energy in Bennett's work, to be sure, but it isn't clear what analytic purpose this energy serves because beyond the marvellous juxtapositions it enables her to conjure there is no theory of combination underpinning it or explaining it. As such, there is no way to distinguish between Bennett's people, insects, odours, ink, electrical flows, air currents, caffeine, tables, chairs, fluids, sounds and so on, and my own completely random collocation of words which follows: frogs, flowers, nuclear energy, alcohol, beds, campervans and so on. It is not the items or elements in the assemblage that is decisive; it is the underlying principles of selection and arrangement that matter and Bennett does not deal with this. I often think the unconscious appeal of vital materialism is that it creates the opportunity and a legitimate reason for people who normally spend their time thinking and writing about intangible things such as concepts and ideas to think and write about tangible, material things. It may well be that because it serves this *writerly* purpose (in Barthes's sense) so well the questions it raises are left to one side lest they interrupt the flow ... people, insects, odours, ink, electrical flows, air currents, caffeine, tables, chairs, fluids, sounds and so on. Certainly no prior history or critical account of existialism has ever known such freedom to range across such diverse materials and write such vivid sentences as the vital materialists permit themselves to write.

Whenever I read vital materialist work I am always reminded of Fredric Jameson's suggestion that the anthropological components of Adorno's work was the 'content [he] had to talk himself into in order to write vivid sentences' and that as such we can understand it in Russian Formalist terms as a '"motivation of the device", a belief that justifies your own aesthetic after the fact.'[6] I am tempted to say something similar is going on in vital materialism because despite its constant emphasis on the vital it is a remarkably lifeless theory, albeit one that is capable of generating lively sentences. At its heart it is a strangely linear kind of adding machine, which like something out of Kafka creates sentences by flattening everything onto a single plane and combining them in an additive fashion: people + insects + odours + ink + electrical flows + air currents + caffeine + tables +chairs + fluids + sounds + so on without limit. Bennett does not propose a power of selection governing the assemblage so it is impossible to say what (if any) difference it might make if one were to either add or subtract one or several variables. Would existialism have arisen if Sartre and his cohort used laptops instead of pen and paper? By contrast, Deleuze and Guattari are very clear that one can neither add nor subtract from the multiplicity that is the assemblage without changing it; they are also clear that there is an underpinning power of selection at work (the body without organs).[7] Moreover the assemblage always has a principle of unity as well (the abstract machine).

The lack of a power of selection creates other, bigger problems. The more widely Bennett ranges in her campaign to compile a comprehensive list of actants to include in her various *catalogues raisonnés* of the assemblages she seeks to document, the further she is compelled to retreat from any direct form of political analysis that might involve laying blame at the feet of a specific individual or set of individuals. Vital materialism, she says, 'does not posit a subject as the root cause of an effect.'[8] The subject, as she sees it, always stands in the middle – figuratively, of course – of a 'swarm of vitalities', so the task of the analyst is to 'identify the contours of the swarm and the kind of relations that obtain between its bits.'[9] Assemblages can have drive, by which she means momentum, but not intentionality or purposiveness, which she acknowledges causes problems for moral philosophy approaches to understanding their actions. If one cannot assign intention then one cannot easily assign either blame or responsibility. But she doesn't stop there. She adds that even the very notion of efficient causality, or billiard-ball causality as she happily calls it, also falters, because there are simply too many variables to consider – the shine of the ball, the quality of the beize and so on. 'Instead of an effect obedient to a determinant, one finds circuits in which effect and cause alternate position and redound on each other.'[10]

Following Arendt, Bennett rejects the utility of the concept of causation for political philosophy in favour of origin, which is conceived as an indeterminate moment when certain trajectories begin to become noticeable. We cannot know in advance what will touch off a particular event or chain of circumstances – the rise of fascism, say, which is Arendt's concern – but we can only determine it retroactively by plotting the 'contingent coming together of a set of elements.'[11] But as we see in her discussion of the possible origins of a large-scale power blackout, her analysis does not interrogate either how the various elements of the assemblage came together or how they interacted to produce the situation she purports to analyse. It seems the more things she identifies that we need to think about in trying to understand a particular assemblage the less able she is to actually analyse it because the elements under consideration are too numerous and too disparate. Without some kind of critical hierarchy mapping of the dependencies between elements in an assemblage (as Hejlmslev advises), all one has is an ever-growing heap of fragments. This is a tension that runs throughout Bennett's account of vital materialism. Bennett acknowledges that her theory limits the degree to which blame can be assigned – she nonetheless regards this as a positive outcome of her model – but argues that it does not mean one has to stop looking for the various avenues by which harmful effects materialize in the present. Bennett's model of thinking invites us to cast our net widely and trawl for literally the most minute actors as well as the unignorably large varieties.

> Look to long-term strings of events: to selfish intentions, to energy policy offering lucrative opportunities for energy trading while generating a tragedy for the commons, and to a psychic resistance to acknowledging a link between American energy use, American imperialism, and Anti-Americanism; but also look to the stubborn directionality of a high-consumption social infrastructure, to unstable electron flows, to conative wildfires, to exurban housing pressures, and to the assemblages they form.[12]

One can easily imagine that all these leads are useful ones, but that is only because other modes of researching and investigating our contemporary situation have already adduced them. However, we are still faced with the question of what should or can one say about these potential sources of harmful effects given that 'vibrant matter presents individuals as simply incapable of bearing *full* responsibility for their effects.'[13] She says, if we inspect assemblages closely, the productive power – the *shi* – will turn out to be a 'confederacy, and the human actants within it will themselves turn out to be confederations of tools, microbes, minerals, sounds, and other "foreign" materialities. Human intentionality can emerge as agentic only by way of such a distribution.'[14] She readily acknowledges that this 'federation of actants is a creature that the concept of moral responsibility fits only loosely and to which the charge of blame will not quite stick.'[15] In fact, she is willing to go further than that and state there is 'no agency proper to assemblages, only the effervescence of the agency of individuals acting alone or in concert with each other.'[16]

One is reminded here of Michaux's description of a 'schizophrenic table', which Deleuze and Guattari cite as emblematic of the process of production of schizophrenic desire. 'The striking thing was that it was neither simple nor really complex, initially or intentionally complex, or constructed according to a complicated plan. Instead, it had been desimplified in the course of carpentering. ... As it stood, it was a table of additions, much like certain schizophrenics' drawings, described as "overstuffed", and if finished it was only in so far as there was no way of adding anything more to it, the table having become more and more an accumulation, less and less a table. ... There was something stunned about it, something petrified. Perhaps suggesting a stalled engine.'[17] That's more or less Bennett's own conclusion too. She says, although it would give her 'pleasure to assert that deregulation and corporate greed are the real culprits in the blackout, the most I can honestly affirm is that corporations are one of the sites at which human efforts at reform can be applied'.[18] Her approach is, in the end, paralysing rather than enabling, because the closer she tries to get to the thing she wants to investigate the further she pushes it away by multiplying endlessly the variables under consideration. The paradox of Bennett's model of the assemblage is that despite its capaciousness it is conceptually one-dimensional – everything, regardless of what it is or how it functions is combined in the same way. Even more problematically, there are no cutting edges in her account of the assemblage, no way to limit them historically, geographically or even physically. Everything is interconnected for Bennett but without any sense of how they are interconnected, which means we are condemned to go on untangling and following threads literally forever without ever being able to decide 'this is it!' A bullet fired from the barrel of a gun connects with the human body very differently than does the sun's rays, so the way things connect is perhaps the most material question of them all and yet any consideration of it is completely absent from Bennett. In this sense it really is like the 'bad' form of schizophrenia Deleuze and Guattari see embodied in the table Michaux describes because all it can do is combine components additively.

In order to avoid this fate, we need to remind ourselves that Deleuze and Guattari's version of the concept of the assemblage has multiple dimensions, not just multiple components, and the analytic affordances it offers are only available when we take into account all of its dimensions. As I have reiterated throughout, it has a material dimension (form of content, machinic assemblage etc.) and an expressive dimension (form of expression, collective assemblages of enunication etc.), a principle of unity (abstract machine), and it rests upon a condition of possibility (BwO, plane of immanence, plane of consistency etc.) which is criss-crossed by lines of flight (lines of deterritorialization and reterritorialization). As we have seen above in my examination of Bennett's version of the assemblage, it is not sufficient to simply ennumerate an assemblage's material components because these do not by themselves disclose the assemblage's constitution, much less its purpose or function. One must also ask how these material components are captured by the expressive dimension and inquire too about its principle of unity and its conditions of possibility. This is not to say that Bennett's focus on the material aspects of the assemblage is wrong, but it is to insist that it is incomplete because it only deals with one aspect of the assemblage. By ignoring its other dimensions Bennett's model leaves itself unable to answer the many questions its investigations into the material aspects of the assemblage raises. In order to illustrate what I mean I am going to offer two brief case studies: the first one is about public housing for indigenous people in Australia and the second one is about the escalating rate of imprisonment in the United States. For the first case, I draw on the work of Tess Lea, an Australian anthropologist with a very keen sense of the importance of the material aspects of the assemblage (my word not hers), but who nevertheless mobilizes her analyses of the material in order to raise questions in the expressive sphere. And for the second case, I turn to the work of Löic Wacquant, a French but US-based sociologist, with a very keen sense of the importance of the expressive aspects of the assemblage (my word not his), but who nevertheless mobilizes his analyses of the expressive in order to raise questions about the material sphere.

I am particularly interested in Lea's work on indigenous housing policy because of the very detailed way she analyses the actual material (right down to the pH of the water) used in the construction of public housing for indigenous people in Australia. Lea does not simply identify which materials are implicated by an assemblage; she asks why are they there, what other materials might have been chosen in their place and what does it tell us about the political nature of the assemblage that these materials were selected? In doing so, she shows that these materials raise conceptual questions that challenge us to rethink the ontology of such apparently straightforward things as the house. This, in turn, challenges us to rethink the ontology of housing policy. In doing so, we move between all the principle working parts of the assemblage, from its machinic material side (actual houses) to its techno-semiotic expressive side (the policy that guides their construction) and from there to the principle of unity (abstract machine) and its condition of possibility (BwO). Lea's analysis is organized around a single but extremely powerful question: When is a house not a house? In Deleuze and Guattari's terms, Lea's question can be understood as an inquiry into the limits of variation that a specific assemblage is capable of. The essential insight of the concept of deterritorialization is that the organizing structure of the assemblage is (to borrow a useful formulation from Jameson) at once *that which allows for maximum variation and that which itself resists all variation.*[19] It is in this precise sense a singularity at the heart of a multiplicity. It has both an internal limit and an external limit, that is, boundaries which cannot be crossed without it becoming something different from what it was. The internal limit refers to the sum total of possible variations it can accommodate; while the external limit refers to the restrictions history itself places on the number of possible variations. Analysis consists of bringing these limits to light.

Public housing (good and bad), like all forms of infrastructure, is the product of countless small and large decisions made by many thousands of people over many decades. Those decisions, however well-intentioned and well thought-through, are not made in a vacuum. Of necessity, they are made in a context defined by a set of constraints (internal and external limits) to do with labour and material costs, existing infrastructure, topography, trade agreements and countless other factors too numerous to even attempt to tabulate here, which ultimately blurs the line between the intended and the unintended, the fated and the accidental. The result is a curious state of affairs which is neither the product of deliberate, conscious design nor the product of random, ad hoc experiments but somehow a combination of these two processes. It is, in this sense, a highly unstable object that requires a supple methodology to grasp and analyse it. To begin with, and perhaps most importantly, we have to stop thinking of infrastructure and infrastructure policy (and indeed all forms of policy) in teleological terms because despite appearances it has neither a clear-cut beginning nor a clear-cut ending.[20] This means, too, we cannot treat policy as a straightforward blueprint for the future. What is proposed and what is delivered is very rarely the same thing. As all project managers know, the delivery of projects rarely follows a prescribed path but has to constantly deal with the unexpected, which in turn tests both the internal and external limits of the overall assemblage. No policy can anticipate all the possible exigencies and contingencies that crop up once building is under way. So rather than conceive policy as a static model which guides the construction of specific pieces of infrastructure, Lea argues that 'policy is an organic – or ..., a *wild* – force, a biota which thrives on the heralding of cataclysms and thus the cumulative need for policy beneficence.'[21]

I like this notion of wild policy because of the impromptu, seat-of-the-pants policy-on-the-fly image it conjures up that goes well beyond the rather too static, feedback loop model of 'formulation-implementation-reformulation' overtly Deleuzian scholars like DeLanda suggest as a means of accommodating the widely acknowledged 'gap' between policy formulation (what policy proposes) and implementation (what is actually delivered). DeLanda says this model works – for his purposes – because it allows for fluidity in the policy-implementation process but still retains the possibility of assessing outcomes.[22] This assumes, however, that policy can be understood in terms of intention, something that Lea challenges, because it treats implementation as the simple execution of a command. This way of seeing policy succumbs to what literary theorists refer to as the 'intentional fallacy' because it holds to the idea that a policy outcome can and should be measured against a policy intention. In literary criticism this position was refuted in two ways: first, the originators of the concept of 'intentional fallacy', W. K. Wimsatt and Monroe Beardsley argued that the actual intention of an author is irrelevant to any evaluation we might make of a work – whether an author set out to compose great poetry or not is irrelevant to the judgement of whether or not their work is in fact great poetry; second, subsequent commentators (particularly those working within a psychoanalytically influenced poststructuralist framework) have added that it is impossible in any case to actually know an author's actual intentions in producing a work. Whether policy architects intend to create good quality housing is equally irrelevant to any judgement we might make of the quality of the housing that is actually built – if the roofs leak and the toilets don't flush then it hardly matters whether this was intended or not because one can adjudge the quality to be poor on those facts alone. Similarly, we cannot really know the intention of policy architects – we may assume they are well-meaning and that they really intend to build good quality housing but somehow failed, and now the roofs leak and the toilets don't flush, but it is only an assumption.

It is equally possible that they had no such intention; that in fact the shoddy housing that was delivered was their actual intention all along, perhaps because they were corrupt or acting out a hidden political agenda. What appears to have been a failure to inhabitants and outside observers may well be viewed as a success by policy insiders who never intended to deliver any better quality than they did. Leaking roofs and non-functioning toilets are signs of success if your intention was to skim the budget, cut costs or deliberately build substandard homes in order to satisfy a political agenda that had nothing to do with the quality of the lives of the people destined to live in the housing you build. As Lea argues, we have to dispense with the fantasy (implicit in the formulation DeLanda adopts) that policy can be thought in systemic terms and evaluated by wiser critics after the fact, assessing what has worked and what hasn't as though intentions are both transparent and benign. To think this way is to remain trapped inside the logic of the system being critiqued and condemn oneself to such self-deceiving platitudes as the idea that in order to improve policy outcomes all one needs to do is improve policy, and that better planning automatically leads to better building. As Lea's work demonstrates, the 'formulation-implementation-reformulation' model is *intrinsic to policy's own idea of itself*, which in Deleuzian terms means it is policy's 'image of thought'.[23] In their self-reflexive moments – that is, in the course of the perennial 'policy review' that accompanies all policy work these days as policy's way of reassuring itself that it isn't drawing its own eye (to borrow a marvellously apt phrase from Jameson) – policy architects are sometimes willing to admit that things haven't gone quite as planned, but Lea argues even this is more self-deception because the 'idea of intentions gone awry pretends there was no foundational opacity within original policy forecasts'.[24] Here then we can see the analytic advantage of the assemblage model, which as I have shown throughout treats the material realm (actual construction) and the discursive realm (policy) as separate and interacting but also autonomous. There is no straight line of causality between them.

How should this model of the assemblage be applied? The 'preferred method' Deleuze and Guattari write, 'would be severely restrictive', by which they mean we should (a) seek to determine the specific conditions under which matter becomes material (i.e. how bricks, timber and steel are determined to be the proper material for housing as opposed to mud, straw and wrecked cars or any other material deemed unsuited to house-building in Australia); (b) seek to determine the specific conditions under which semiotic matter becomes expressive (i.e. how it is decided that a specific arrangement of materials is 'fitting' for a person to live in and another arrangement is not).[25] Here I must clarify that for Deleuze and Guattari expression, or better yet 'becoming expressive', does not mean simply that something has acquired meaning(s) in the semiotic sense; rather, it refers to the fact it has a performative function. It is clear that the word 'indigenous', for example, has a performative as well as a semiotic function (indeed the latter is in all likelihood an epiphenomenon of the former). As Lea's analyses make abundantly apparent, the assemblage 'indigenous housing' is very different in its formulation to what we might think of as 'regular housing' (a phrase I use purely for convenience without any wish to defend it).

To conceive of policy as an assemblage means seeing it in terms of the kinds of arrangements and orderings it makes possible and even more importantly the complex and not always fully disclosed set of expectations it entails. To see it this way we need to separate 'policy' as a conceptual entity from its myriad iterations as this or that policy, for example, infrastructure policy, health policy, transport policy and so on, but also from all sense of outcomes and outputs. We also have to see so-called policy decisions as components of the policy assemblage and not as some kind of climactic moment in the life of a policy. Policy decisions are part of the form of expression of the policy assemblage, not the content. By questioning the very idea of policy Lea has enabled us to see it in its properly rhizomatic light. As Lea shows, policymaking takes place 'in the middle of things' but always pretends otherwise because it is locked into an image of itself as a special type of agency that defines and measures 'progress'. When policy looks at itself it only sees beginnings and endings, starting points that lack intentionality (a situation that stands in need of rectification) and finishing points that are fully intended (a changed situation). In the middle is action and though policy claims to function as a guide to what happens it eschews all responsibility.

Lea's ethnography of the debate that went on behind closed doors in the implementation phase of Australia's Strategic Indigenous Housing and Infrastructure Program (SIHIP) offers a real-world example of 'wild policy' at work in the organizing structure of the indigenous housing assemblage. Launched in 2009 with considerable fanfare and a seemingly bottomless well of money, the SIHIP was supposed to 'fix' long-identified problems in indigenous housing in northern Australia. With a budget of almost $AUS 950 million, the programme as it was publicly announced was intended to provide 750 new houses and refurbishment of a further 2,500 houses for indigenous people in seventy-three communities across the Northern Territory (NT). To put this into perspective, it needs to be borne in mind that in terms of surface area the NT is twice the size of that famously big place Texas, it is bigger even than South Africa, and it is six times greater than Great Britain, and it only has a population of a little over 200,000. To say it is sparsely populated is an understatement. Outside its three main cities, which account for over third of its population, the small settlements, farms and communities are defined by their remoteness and isolation. Health care is delivered by airplane because the distances are so great – measured in hours of flying, days of driving, rather than kilometres, reflecting the fact that literally nothing is close by. Perhaps unsurprisingly, then, given the scale of the NT, the SIHIP ran into serious budgetary problems from the very beginning as original cost estimates proved to be well short of actual costs; this problem was in turn compounded by blatant corruption on the part of 'white' building contractors, who rapidly turned the whole thing into a boondoggle for themselves. It was a public relations disaster for the government because the constant rorting of the programme pushed up the unit cost of the individual houses to the point where 'urban' Australians (i.e. 'white' middle-class voting Australians) began to express resentment at the amount of money being spent on building houses for 'black' people living in the 'bush'. The build cost of houses in remote parts of Australia is so high that even modest homes are extremely expensive and by implication appear to be 'luxurious' and 'undeserved' to uneducated urban eyes.

The blatant undercurrent of racism fuelling the national outburst of *ressentiment* the SIHIP fiasco occasioned was all too obvious, but what was less obvious was the way this racism manifested itself in policy discussions. As Lea amply documents, racism finds its purest and most baleful expression in ontology. In order to bring costs down and get the whole mess out of the media spotlight the politicians and senior bureaucrats charged with 'fixing' things invited the building contractors who had hitherto 'failed' to deliver appropriately costed houses to reconsider the very meaning and actual substance of the concept of a house. Behind closed doors the builders were told 'everything is on the table'.

With ... the invitation to 'put it on the table,' the discussion quickly turned to ways of building lower-cost houses at speed by lopping off such seemingly discretionary design features as louvered windows and sunhoods, internal flashings for waterproofing, or disabled access. In the flurry of designing and then undoing the designs for appropriate housing, it was the sound of a built house falling apart in the non-specifiable future that could not compete with the noise of a threatened-and-defensive government in the here and now.[26]

By putting literally 'everything on the table' the government effectively gave the builders a free hand to determine not only what constitutes indigenous housing in the ontological sense (thus redefining its internal limits) but also what constitutes an appropriate dwelling for an indigenous person in an actual material sense (thus redefining its external limits). But, she asks, is a house still a house if – as was often the case with the houses built under the auspices of SIHIP – it isn't connected to water? Is it still a house if it doesn't have adequate temperature control or any means of cooling it down in the year round hot weather northern Australia experiences? Is it still a house if the sewage pipes are not connected to a sewage system?[27] These are the internal limits of the housing assemblage and under normal circumstances it would be impossible to ignore these limits and still call the result a house. But in this instance with all the rules quite consciously suspended a new assemblage was brought into being.

The assemblage question is: According to what criteria is it acceptable and legitimate to not only build houses of this materially substandard variety but also to expect the intended occupants to not only live in them but express gratitude for the 'privilege'? This question cannot be answered unless we look further afield than the materials themselves. Lea uses the actual materiality of matter in the most literal and granular sense in a dialectical fashion to expose the fault lines in the expressive dimension. By examining in detail the physical and chemical properties of water, for example, and its implications for building houses in tropical locations (form of content), she exposes the critical shallowness of policy thinking which is more focused on ticking boxes than it is in creating enduring, liveable houses in the material sphere (form of expression). There are two separate processes at work here: on the one hand, there is a set of questions about what constitutes a house in a material-semiotic sense, which corresponds to the internal limit of the assemblage; on the other hand, there is a set of questions about what constitutes an appropriate dwelling in an ethico-political sense, which corresponds to the external limit of the assemblage. By looking at the 'house' in this way, as an assemblage that is the product of highly specific choices and decisions, our attention is directed in a very particular way: it asks us to reverse the usual way of seeing material – material isn't, on this view of things, merely a condition of possibility, as it tends to be in most so-called 'new materialist' accounts; rather, it is anything which can be interpolated and accommodated by the expressive sphere. Material must always be produced; it doesn't simply exist.[28] We have to resist the empiricist tendency to treat material as given and instead ask the more properly transcendental-empiricist question: How and under what conditions does matter become material?

In an Australian context, bricks, timber, pressed iron and fibreboard all seem like 'proper' materials for house-building, whereas mud, straw, bark, plastic bottles and car bodies do not. But in fact there is no intrinsic reason why these 'other' materials should be excluded tout court. At various times in Australia's colonial history, houses made from mud, straw, bark and roughly hewn tree branches were regarded by the country's European settlers as perfectly fine, albeit provisional modes of housing. Indeed, they were seen as distinctly 'above' the accommodation indigenous peoples deemed suitable to their own needs. Now, though, such constructions are deemed archaic, unsuited to the needs of contemporary existence. In this way, matter is made to bear the weight of history and the myth of progress. Deleuze and Guattari's question is: What are the limits to what can and cannot be counted as material for a particular assemblage and how are these limits decided? The implication is that one cannot look to the material itself to find the answer; instead, one has to examine the assemblage as a whole – what are its requirements? What expectations does it create? What are the tensions internal to it? This in turn leads us to the external limit and the role 'history' itself plays in shaping what can and cannot become the proper material of an actant. Now the issue is less what material is suitable for house-building and more what material is 'fitting', where 'fitting' is an ethico-political judgement about what kinds of houses people 'ought' to live in.

That these two formalizations are arbitrary and mobile can be seen in the fact that both vary considerably from country to country and more especially from one class perspective to another. The modest suburban home is a mansion to the slum-dweller, and the slum-dweller's shanty is a mansion to the rough-sleeper who spends their nights huddled in cardboard lean-tos; by the same token, the suburban home is 'fitting' for a middle-class 'white' person, just as the shanty is – in the eyes of that same middle-class 'white' person – 'fitting' for a poor person, particularly one living in a remote part of the country where they are literally out of sight and out of mind. Formalization means there is a unity of composition, or to put it another way there is an underlying principle of inclusion and exclusion. But the principle of inclusion and exclusion for one dimension (content) can and often is in conflict with the principle of inclusion and exclusion for the other dimension (expression). But what is of central importance – and the reason why the assemblage is such a powerful concept – is the question of what it takes to yoke together these two dimensions in the first place: *this* is what the assemblage does. We have to stop thinking of the concept of the assemblage as a way of describing a thing or situation and instead see it for what it was always intended to be, a way of analysing a thing or situation. Faced with any apparent assemblage we should ask, what holds it together? What are its limits (internal and external) and what function does it fulfil?

Now I want to turn to Wacquant's work on imprisonment in the United States, specifically his book *Punishing the Poor*, which is to my mind one of the finest examples of assemblage theory at work, and it does not even mention Deleuze and Guattari. It is fitting that we should focus on prisons for the second case study because the key 'real world' illustration of the assemblage understood as the doubly articulated relation between form of content and form of expression that Deleuze and Guattari offer is culled from Michel Foucault's analysis of prisons in *Discipline and Punish*. 'Take a thing like the prison: the prison is a form, "the prison-form"; it is a form of content on a stratum and is related to other forms of content (school, barracks, hospital, factory etc.). This thing does not refer back to the word "prison" but to entirely different words and concepts, such as "delinquent" and "delinquency", which express a new way of classifying, stating, translating and even committing criminal acts. "Delinquency" is the form of expression in reciprocal presupposition with the form of content "prison".'[29] The form of content is not a thing, it is not a specific building known as a prison; it is rather, a complex state of affairs, a formation of power, which ultimately points to a regime that operates by incarcerating certain types of people. The prison is not merely an apparatus or instrument used by a given society to deal with a specific problem; it is a symptom of that society's concern (or not) for the welfare of its entire population. The one who supports incarceration is just as much a part of the 'carceral society' as the incarcerated; indeed, one might say they are the only ones who are part of the 'carceral society' since their support is given by choice. The form of expression is similarly not just a set of signifiers or a related text, as it were, but an autonomous body of discourse, that defines, classifies and evaluates crimes. Deleuze and Guattari will go so far as to say it even invents ways of committing crimes. Foucault's work shows that neither the idea of imprisonment nor the reasons for which people are imprisoned unfolded according to an evolutionary model.

Löic Wacquant shows that the prison is foremost an instrument of state power whose main purpose is to preserve the power of the ruling elite, not simply by incarcerating people who violate state laws but by *being seen* to incarcerate people who violate state laws. Although Wacquant does not draw on Deleuze and Guattari, his approach bears a striking resemblance to theirs because of the way he combines the materialist analyses of Marx (form of content) with the symbolic analyses of Weber and Bourdieu (form of expression). He similarly treats the prison system and the notion of delinquency as a separate but interlocking formations of forces. The materialist perspective focuses on the changing relations between the prison system and the economy; the symbolic perspective focuses on the way the state tries to produce social reality by means of its classifications and categories. In criminology and sociology these two approaches have generally regarded each other with hostility, but as Wacquant puts it this is just an accident of history because the historical reality is that the prison system both enforces control and communicates social norms. 'The prison symbolizes material divisions and materializes relations of symbolic power; its operation ties together inequality and identity, fuses domination and signification, and welds the passions and the interests that traverse and roil society.'[30] The prison is simultaneously a machine for warehousing the poor, the politically disenfranchised, the discarded and excluded of society and at the same time an ideological instrument that reassures the anxious middle classes that not only is their life and property being made secure by these means, but their symbolic position as the 'deserving' class is also being safeguarded.[31]

The current worldwide explosion in penality, by which I mean not just the expansion of the prison system but also the expansion of the idea that imprisonment is the only valid solution to social problems as varied as petty criminals and asylum seekers, was neither predicted nor inevitable. As Wacquant observes, in the early 1970s (i.e. before Nixon made the fateful move of declaring war 'on drugs') leading historians and sociologists of the prison system such as Michel Foucault and Stanley Cohen agreed that the prison system was in decline.[32] Yet, in the United States at least, precisely the opposite happened – there was a major reversal, from a steady decline of prisoner numbers through the 1960s to an exponential uptick in numbers through the 1970s to the present, such that the United States has become a genuinely carceral society with over 2 million people imprisoned (in 1975 it was 380,000).[33] The 'war on drugs' is usually blamed for this massive growth in prisoner numbers and indeed a substantial proportion of the prison population are convicted of drug-related crimes, but this still leaves unanswered the more important question of why declare war on drugs in the first place. Drug use was in steady decline at the time of the declaration, so there was no strong imperative or need to militarize the problem (assuming one agrees with the state's assessment that drug use *is* a problem).[34] And it was already well established in government circles that imprisonment was the least effective means of addressing the issue.[35] The state had other options up its sleeve that were already well established: (1) *socialization* – address it as a structural problem that can be remediated by building low-cost housing, providing training and creating jobs for the poor, particularly the urban poor; (2) *medicalization* – address it as a public health issue that can be remediated by building rehab centres and mental health facilities, providing access to free healthcare and making available addiction treatment. Instead, the state chose option (3) penalization – the production of delinquency as a personal problem that the state has no responsibility to assist with, only the duty to contain.[36]

In an exemplary move, Wacquant argues that we cannot understand the prison system by focusing solely on enclosed world of prisons and prisoners, we need to pull back and look at the stratum as a whole (not his choice of words, obviously), which in this instance means factoring in what is happening more broadly at the level of the state. At this level it is immediately clear that neither drugs nor criminality nor even poverty were ever the main problem as far as the state is concerned. The real issue was elsewhere. Wacquant identifies the ascendency of neoliberalism as the main culprit because it placed the state in the strange position of having to give up all its roles and responsibilities except its right to exercise and control violence. As the state acceded to the demands of 'big business' for a 'free market', which in practice meant the right of corporations to take back the commons, and retreated from its many 'caring' roles and responsibilities such as welfare, pensions, education, healthcare, public housing, the provision of utilities (e.g. power and water), and the building and maintenance of infrastructure, allowing all of these essential components of modern society to become (if they weren't already) privately owned and therefore profit-making, it found that its only remaining source of moral legitimacy was its security services. If it no longer cares for its populace by supporting them through the provision of welfare and the guarantee of a good life, then the only way the state can show it cares for its people and therefore has a moral right to continue to exist is by removing the velvet glove from its chainmailed fist and showing the people that it can protect them from the desperadoes its policies create. This process has taken a number of forms, but undoubtedly the most important manifestation has been the relentless drive to demonize poverty *as* dependency and make all recipients of state support (of whatever variety) appear not merely socially inferior but criminal.[37] Through clampdowns on so-called 'benefit fraud' and 'work for the dole' schemes both the left and the right sides of government in virtually every country have stigmatized welfare recipients as parasites who deserve to be punished. This in turn begs the question: How did 'our' middle-class hearts become so hardened that we would rather vote for the party that promises to punish the poor than the one that promises to help the poor to thrive? The catalogue of horrors documented by Wacquant shows very clearly that the prison industrial complex as it is often called would not function as it does without an accompanying and constantly evolving regime of signs to support it.

5

Control Assemblage

In this concluding chapter I want to revisit Deleuze's essay 'Postscript on Control Societies' (Post-Scriptum sur les Sociétés des Contrôle) for two reasons: first, because it is one of the most incisive pieces of work Deleuze wrote about our contemporary situation; and second, because the significance of the concept of the assemblage to this piece of work is generally overlooked. Moreover as one of his later pieces, I tend to think of it as the preliminary sketch of a future and alas never to be completed project, perhaps even a third volume of the Capitalism and Schizophrenia series, which would have made more explicit just how he and Guattari envisaged deploying the concept of the assemblage in their analyses of the present. I suspect too that this essay contains the seeds of Deleuze's well-known and much-lamented great unfinished project on the 'greatness of Marx'. All of this is pure speculation on my part, but I tend to think that if there is a trend in Deleuze's final publications it is in the direction of an analysis of control societies and not as Agamben speculates in the direction of an analysis of 'life' as pure immanence.[1] I take my cue here from the following passage, in which Deleuze lays out what he sees as the essential critical task of our moment. He says, 'We ought to establish the basic sociotechnological principles of control mechanisms as their age dawns, and describe in these terms what is already taking the place of disciplinary sites of confinement that everyone says are breaking down.'[2] He might just as well have said we ought to discover the assemblages underpinning and driving contemporary control society as its age dawns because that is precisely what is meant by the phrase 'sociotechnological principles'. It combines the two basic elements of the assemblage: the machinic (technological) and the expressive (socio).

Deleuze foresaw to a remarkable degree the emerging diagram of our time. He mapped in the span of a handful of pages one of the most searing diagnoses of our situation critical theory has produced. This is not to say that this essay is only of value insofar as it is predictive, which is an impossible benchmark for even the greatest of prognosticians to have to live up to. It seems to me that the best way to read Deleuze's essay is as a partial, ongoing, still-to-be-completed analysis of the present, and not as the prediction of a dystopia we're all doomed to endure like some toxic postcard from the past (e.g. the Biff character in *Back to the Future II* modelled on Donald Trump). Admittedly Deleuze's description of control society as a new monster arising from the ashes of Foucault's disciplinary society, not to mention the fact he appropriates the word 'control' from the paranoid world of William S. Burroughs, does give it a distinctly dystopian hue. But that doesn't mean it should be read as dystopian, which to-date has been the (almost) default way of reading it. The trouble with dystopias, as Jameson has argued, is that they tend to be politically conservative (which Deleuze decidedly was not) in that they predict doom as a just punishment for the failings of human character, and more problematically still, they are never far away from becoming anti-utopian (which Deleuze also decidedly was not).[3]

As Deleuze noted, most of the first world nations have moved in the decades since the end of the Second World War from an essentially stable binary politics of the left and the right to a multidimensional and metastable politics of the centre (defined very approximately as an unwillingness to openly support labour combined with a reticence to openly admit that serving big business is the primary mission – in the age of Trump this reticence is steadily turning into its opposite and big business boosterism is becoming not only more blatant but also more legitimate). Political conviction has been replaced by a politicized form of affect which gives the same political weight to inchoate feelings and emotions that was once reserved for reasoned positions built around the question of class interest. As the clustered elections of Donald Trump (USA), Jair Bolsanaro (Brazil), Boris Johnson (UK) and Scott Morrison (Australia) demonstrate, workers today seem to identify with mercurial figures who in previous decades would have been viewed as both unworthy of office and a living symbol of the oppression of workers. In part this is because the increasingly deunionized workers of today have bought into (willingly or not) the neoliberal doctrine that the enrichment of the few is the key to the prosperity of the many, despite the abundance of social and economic evidence to the contrary. Class anxiety and the perpetual fear of downward mobility are undoubtedly crucial factors (as Klein and others point out[4]) in creating the political climate in which somebody like Trump could get elected, but following Deleuze I would argue these are surface effects of a deeper phenomenon, namely the destabilization of the old political hierarchies which once demarcated cleanly between owners of the means of production and wage earners, which Deleuze calls *modulation*.

Deleuze's argument is that during the course of the twentieth century the world entered a new epoch, one that is differently organized to the world Foucault mapped in his work on disciplinary society. There has been considerable, but I think rather needless debate as to whether we have left disciplinary society behind completely or not.[5] The debate is needless because Deleuze never claims that the machinery of disciplinary society has disappeared altogether; he claims only that it has broken down and been superseded by new machineries of control. That this is the case is manifestly obvious. While no one can dispute that surveillance technology continues to dominate twenty-first-century life, as Foucault said it did in the centuries preceding our own, it is also true that surveillance today operates in ways that were not technologically possible prior to the invention of the computer. Not only that, its very modality has changed too. Today surveillance is focused on controlling dividuals (not individuals), restricting their movement, limiting their access to credit and capital, determining where and how they can spend their money, and not, as was the case with disciplinary society, in shaping and forming them as particular social types (soldiers, doctors, teachers and so on). Discipline concerned the correct training and placement of individuals, whereas control is concerned with the maximum exploitation of dividuals (nameless, faceless, data points) regardless of their formation or placement. It is clear too that control society regards humans as replaceable – the machines of today do not merely extend or enhance human capabilities, they substitute for them, and in many cases do the job better than any human could.

The more we come to understand the power of corporations like Google and Facebook the more we realize that there is still so much they could and probably will do to infiltrate, shape and ultimately monetize our daily lives.[6] Evidence of this shift in priority is not hard to find. Jerry Muller's *The Tyranny of Metrics* provides a litany of examples attesting to this point but perhaps none more telling or more cruelly absurd than the following. A hospital in New York State wanted to improve the post-operative survival rates of its coronary bypass patients so it introduced a 'report card' for all its surgeons, comparing the mortality rates of their respective patients. The idea, evidently, was that by creating competition between surgeons they would be encouraged to improve their performance and save more lives in the process. Sure enough, mortality rates did decline, but further investigation revealed several unintended effects: first, surgeons began to decline to operate on patients deemed high risk because it might adversely affect their scorecard, so patients who might otherwise have been given a chance at better health, or indeed a longer life, missed out; second, when operations weren't successful doctors kept their patients on life support for thirty days so that they wouldn't die within the time frame their scorecards measured and thereby bring their stats down. The net cost of this experiment to the hospital, not to mention the patients and their families, far outweighed any benefit it might conceivably have obtained. Symptomatically, it revealed a willingness to put trust into non-human systems at the expense of more humane (and human) practices. The scorecard is a control measure rather than a disciplinary measure because it does not seek to train surgeons (individuals), to improve or correct their technique, only to measure a particular output, and record a particular statistic (dividuals). The hospital machine determined whether it was working well or not according to this data, rather than any assessment of the actual health and well-being of its patients, or any assessment of the relative skill, learning and innovativeness of its surgeons involved.[7]

It is important to see here that this (increasingly common) turn towards so-called performance indicators as a means of managing people is not simply an intensification of Foucault's discipline but a change in the way society thinks about and organizes itself. Confinement has broken down because new technology has facilitated vastly more intrusive and exploitative forms of what I will call open capture. This amounts to a new iteration of primitive accumulation that treats culture – or more specifically cultural practices – in the same way extractive capitalism treats nature.[8]

> Larry Page [Google's co-founder] grasped that human experience could be Google's virgin wood, that it could be extracted at no extra cost online and at very low cost out in the real world. For today's owners of surveillance capital the experiential realities of bodies, thoughts and feelings are as virgin and blameless as nature's once-plentiful meadows, rivers, oceans and forests before they fell to the market dynamic. We have no formal control over these processes because we are not essential to the new market action. Instead *we are exiles from our own behaviour*, denied access to or control over knowledge derived from its dispossession by others for others. Knowledge, authority and power rest with surveillance capital, for which we are merely 'human natural resources'. We are the native peoples now whose claims to self-determination have vanished from the maps of our own experience.[9]

Exiles from our behaviour, this articulates perfectly the epochal change Deleuze wanted to alert us to thirty years ago – we are no longer primarily consumers (i.e. individuals who exercise their judgement to purchase products and services), we have become the raw materials out of which digitally focused corporations manufacture their products (i.e. dividuals), which they sell to other corporations interested in further repackaging us. The panopticon Foucault feared so much is child's play compared to the digital technology we are immersed in today, which is unprecedented in history in its capacity as a surveillance device.

We willingly carry surveillance technology (in the form of our smart phones) with us at all times, allowing it to record our every movement, our financial transactions, our health data and even how we feel about a wide variety of subjects. Not only that, we willingly pay for the privilege of giving all our data to private corporations. But as Zuboff argues, corporations like Google and Facebook no longer find it to be 'enough to automate information flows about us', to simply collect our data, their 'goal now is to automate us. [Their] processes are meticulously designed to produce ignorance by circumventing individual awareness and thus eliminate any possibility of self-determination.'[10] As Facebook's infamous 2012 'experiment' on 700,000 of its users to see if it could affect their moods by manipulating their feeds demonstrated digital corporations are both fully aware of their capacity to influence people's behaviour and unafraid, or at any rate not morally opposed, to utilizing this capacity.[11] This became evident following the US election in 2016 when it emerged that the notorious disinformation campaign orchestrated by the now-defunct company Cambridge Analytica had in conjunction with Facebook played a significant hand in helping Trump gain the White House. Facebook's role was so significant that in 2019 it was fined US$5 billion by the US Federal Trade Commission for inappropriately sharing the data of 87 million of its users with Cambridge Analytica, thereby enabling their highly successful project of discrediting Trump's electoral competitors at every stage of the election process.[12] Thanks to Cambridge Analytica the meme 'Crooked Hilary' became a household phrase in the targeted homes of potential Trump voters identified by algorithms responding to 'likes' and 'friends' and her support withered in key states such as Wisconsin which she assumed she would comfortably win and therefore neglected to visit in the lead up to the election.

Facebook is now one of the most important sources of news for hundreds of millions of people, but unlike the fourth estate of old – of legend, perhaps – it has no vested interest in ensuring that the news it circulates is valid and it invests no effort or expense in vetting the material it circulates. Not only that, it does not simply disseminate information as regular news sources do, it distributes it point to point, from one friendship group to another (i.e. from one milieu to another), without ever distinguishing between high quality investigative journalism and so-called 'fake news'. In the process it manufactures ignorance, as Zuboff puts it, because it deprives the news it circulates of the critical context required to understand it and where necessary challenge it. The internet is touted as a resource of unprecedented power when it comes to checking the validity of information, yet it seems it has never been easier for lies and misinformation to wear the veil of truth and fact.

> In the open air, fake news can be debated and exposed; on Facebook, if you aren't a member of the community being served the lies, you're quite likely never to know that they are in circulation. It's crucial to this that *Facebook has no financial interest in telling the truth*. No company better exemplifies the internet-age dictum that if the product is free, you are the product. Facebook's customers aren't the people who are on the site: its customers are the advertisers who use its network and who relish its ability to direct ads to receptive audiences. Why would Facebook care if the news streaming over the site is fake? Its interest is in the targeting, not in the content.[13]

This isn't a new phenomenon. Social media has merely found the means of monetizing a trend that was already apparent when Deleuze was alive. Even then politics was steadily being transformed into a sideshow more concerned with the popularity of specific politicians than their particular policy platforms. Deleuze argues that the evidence for this deep shift in political sensibilities is to be found in plain sight in our popular culture. Deleuze of course meant western popular culture, but in the age of globalized media there is probably no country on earth that is spared the dross that comprises the bread and butter of contemporary media forms (e.g. reality TV, game shows, news, magazine shows, cooking shows etc.). As he puts it, 'If the stupidest TV game shows are successful [and let's not forget that it was literally a stupid TV game show that helped put Trump into the White House], it's because they're a perfect reflection of the way businesses are run' today. In contrast to the old duality of management and trade unions today's businesses 'are constantly introducing an inexorable rivalry presented as healthy competition, a wonderful motivation that sets individuals against one another and sets itself up in each of them, dividing each within himself'.[14] Competition for its own sake lives and thrives on the intermittent highs of transitory victories (e.g. heart surgeon of the month), and never concerns itself with whether or not these victories add up to something meaningful like competency or a vocation. Not even education is immune from this trend, Deleuze laments. Schooling has been replaced 'by *continuing education* and exams by continuous assessment'. To which he adds, showing uncanny prescience: 'It's the surest way of turning education into a business.'[15]

Deleuze's claims about the transformations in capital are congruent with the broad thrust of David Harvey's work, beginning with his landmark book *The Condition of Postmodernity*, which was published in the same year as Deleuze's essay. Like Harvey, Deleuze argues that nineteenth-century capitalism was 'directed towards production', the manufacture of material things, but today it is 'directed towards metaproduction'. Capitalism is no longer premised on buying raw materials and selling finished products. Now, 'it buys finished products or assembles them from parts. What it seeks to sell is services, and what it seeks to buy, activities.'[16] Naomi Klein's *No Logo* offers a detailed account of what this reshaping of the economy looks like on the ground to consumers botanizing in virtual and actual malls and high streets. With a journalist's eye for the 'scoop' she shows that apparel companies like Nike and Benetton are not the clothing manufacturers they appear to be; rather they are purchasers and re-sellers of clothes made by textile companies in low wage zones (often this means so-called 'third world' countries like Bangladesh and Vietnam, but it can also mean the inner third worlds – as Deleuze and Guattari put it – of first world cities like Los Angeles and Naples). What they make is their brand and what they sell is a brand story (as the marketing people say), which is not merely a set of associations that one might make with the objects they sell but a territory one can occupy by power of an attachment to a specific commodity (e.g. Lightning McQueen). Klein's book is driven by a desire to understand how it is possible that people willingly pay several times more for a basic item like a T-shirt just because it has a fashion logo inscribed on it. If she is unable to answer this question with any degree of satisfaction, it is because she relies on a model of desire that assumes that only dupes could fall for such an obvious scam as designer T-shirts. She doesn't take into account the possibility that there might be affirmative reasons why they could want such items.

At the level of the machinic apparatus, the model of capitalism Klein describes is precisely the one Deleuze mapped in his essay – it is driven by metaproduction – but at the level of the assemblage her analysis lacks Deleuze and Guattari's interest in the workings of desire. The shift from disciplinary society to control society is a change in the structure and organization of capitalism precipitated by changes in the collective desire of a particular society. Klein argues that the mobilization of the logo enabled the dematerialization of businesses like Nike, but what she does not explain is the changes in desire that enabled this investment of desire in the logo. One might say then that she focuses on the machines of capitalism at the expense of its expressive dimension. 'One can of course see how each kind of society corresponds to a particular kind of machine – with simple mechanical machines corresponding to sovereign societies, thermodynamic machines to disciplinary societies, cybernetic machines and computers to control societies.' But, he adds, the 'machines don't explain anything' by themselves; 'you have to analyse the collective apparatuses [i.e. assemblages] of which the machines are just one component.'[17] As Deleuze says, setting up these kinds of correspondences between particular machines and types of society is easy, but this doesn't mean the machines determine the nature of the society. Rather, the machines can be understood as expressing 'the social forms capable of producing them and making use of them'.[18] The dot.com bust of the late 1990s demonstrated that digital technology did not automatically create the social and cultural conditions needed for the business ideas it enabled to flourish. In most cases it took at least another decade before people became accustomed to the new affordances the technology offered and trusted them enough to embrace it. It is hard to believe now, but online shopping once seemed fraught with all kinds of risk – largely of fraud – and many people were afraid to try it. Over time, new social forms – trust systems and the like – were engineered to enable people to feel comfortable with the new businesses sprouting like wild grass on the internet.

Deleuze was not a technological determinist. The machines he and Guattari were interested in were never exclusively technological either; they always had a socio-psychological dimension that could not be reduced to a set of physical materials. Capitalism invents and invests in the machines it needs in order to continue to generate and recycle capital, Deleuze argues, but not because the new types of machines that appear periodically are intrinsically better and more productive than their forebears, and certainly not out of any sense of or desire for progress (if that were true we wouldn't be facing the climate catastrophe looming before us), but always with a view to escaping the trap of economic stagnation. For example, the technological underpinnings of the popular music business have advanced considerably in the past few decades from vinyl to CDs to MP3 and beyond that to iTunes and Spotify, but at the same time it has seen its revenues shrink dramatically. The paradox of the music business is that technology has undermined the very foundations of its business model, which until now has been premised on freezing content into a material commodity that is packaged and sold like breakfast cereal. Now content has been volatized by the new digital formats and 'set free' (to use the jargon of the techno-utopians) and made free to obtain, making it almost impossible to capture and control. This is why, as Deleuze and Guattari argue in *Anti-Oedipus*, the flow of capital is always balanced by an equivalent flow of stupidity, which stifles both technical innovation and social and economic revolution. Big corporations are not unaware of the financial perils of innovation, though they are not always able to deal with the consequences in the way they might like. (Kodak is the textbook example of a corporate giant wiped out in less than a generation by technological change.) And it is not just corporations that are bamboozled by technology. Knowledge workers who are well-positioned to grasp the reality of their situations are drawn into a form of 'axiomatized stupidity' by their attraction to their 'gadgets', their iPad and iPhone and so on, which become 'desiring-machines' capturing and curtailing their creativity rather than liberating it as the techno-propagandists promised.[19] Here I'm thinking of the obsession with PowerPoint and Prezi that has swept through academia in the past couple of decades convincing lecturers and students alike that entertainment is the key to education and that banishing boredom is crucial if learning is not to be impeded.[20]

As I have argued throughout, assemblages are double-sided – there is a machinic side and an expressive side. The two sides are mutually presupposed but also autonomous from one another. The machinic side concerns bodies (broadly defined as anything capable of entering into a causal or semi-causal relation with something), while the expressive side concerns the incorporeal transformation of those bodies (broadly this might be understood as the application of labels on those bodies). Zuboff's analysis of what she calls surveillance capitalism offers a vivid illustration of how this works. As she points out, what is particularly striking and indeed alarming about the new surveillance corporations is the fact that they have created a field of operation for themselves that is essentially beyond the reach of law. The power they have 'to shape behaviour for others' profit or power is entirely *self-authorising*. It has no foundation in democratic or moral legitimacy, as it usurps decision rights and erodes the processes of individual autonomy that are essential to the function of a democratic society. The message here is simple: Once I was mine. Now I am theirs.'[21] Deleuze and Guattari argue that this form of *self-authorizing* law-making, which they refer to as axiomatics, is a defining characteristic of contemporary capitalism.

This is the territorializing (expressive) side of the assemblage. The axiomatic is an unfounded rule, it is entirely arbitrary, it isn't based in law, religion, or any grounding form of belief. It just is, but it is also capable of transforming bodies by power of its declaration. This is not to say that Google and Facebook and countless other digital platforms couldn't be regulated, because certainly they could; but it is to say that at present they are given extremely broad discretionary powers to define for themselves what constitutes right and wrong. The very fact that they ask us to agree to waive our rights to privacy, to the ownership of our own content and so on, in order to make use of these platforms, says a great deal about the way they are regulated. One may well wonder what kind of a legal framework allows that a corporation may invade your privacy and take your personal data and sell it for profit just because you as a largely ignorant consumer agree to it.

Still on the expressive side, control society has witnessed a dramatic change in our relation to machines – whereas once we were enslaved by our machines (discipline), now we are subjected to our machines (control); we are not cogs in a megamachine constituting a higher authority – the state, the church, civil society and so on – as we once were, now we are 'connected' to a machine that no longer needs us to function.[22] 'For example, one is subjected to TV insofar as one uses and consumes it, in the very particular situation of a subject of the statement that more or less mistakes itself for a subject of enunciation ("you dear television viewers, who make TV what it is ..."); the technical machine is the medium between two subjects. But one is enslaved by TV as a human machine insofar as the television viewers are no longer consumers or users, nor even subjects who supposedly "make" it, but intrinsic component pieces, "input" and "output", feedback or recurrences that are no longer connected to the machine in such a way as to produce or use it.'[23] Social media constantly positions – flatters – us as users, but at the same time depends on our free labour to function. Every time we post on Facebook or Instagram or their equivalents we are performing free labour because it is our posts that make the sites interesting and attractive to potential users, which in turn creates an audience that the platform can sell to advertisers. But that's not all we do for free in the interest of these new media platforms. We also provide our personal data for free, which includes our movements, travels, purchases and so on, all of which is valuable to marketing companies looking to develop highly specific 'leads' for their products. We also give our attention to our devices and tell ourselves we are using them, even as they are using us, suggesting that in contrast to previous media forms social media combines the exploitative potential of both machinic enslavement and subjectification, making it a far more potent mechanism of 'unfreedom' than anything hitherto witnessed in history.

Our response to the changing nature of our circumstances shouldn't be to inquire whether the older systems were better or worse, rather we should be looking for new weapons.[24]

Notes

Introduction

1 This chapter contains elements (in revised form) that were previously published in Buchanan 2015.

2 Law 2004: 2.

3 Law 2004: 2.

4 Deleuze and Guattari 1994: 28.

5 See DeLanda 2016: 1–7.

6 Jameson 1991: 25.

7 I use 'return' in the Lacanian sense of returning not to a specific text but to the situation that gave rise to the text. For Lacan this was the analytic situation of Freud, his encounter with the other that was his patients. For Deleuze and Guattari the situation is the possibility of revolution.

8 Indeed, the problem is endemic and known to be so. In their 2006 summary of assemblage theory's applications in anthropological research, Marcus and Saka make the following interesting and I suspect quite accurate observation: 'None of the derivations of assemblage from Deleuze and Guattari of which we are aware is based on … a technical and formal analysis of how this concept functions in their writing. Few in the social sciences who have found the modernist sensibilities embedded in the concepts that Deleuze and Guattari deploy for their purposes to be attractive have appreciated, understood or incorporated those purposes in their own. Rather, it has been the power and often beguiling attraction of Deleuze and Guattari's language that has encouraged the piecemeal appropriation of certain concepts for the remaking of middle-range

theorizing that informs contemporary research projects' (Marcus and Saka 2006: 103).

9 Deleuze 1995: 6.

10 Deleuze and Guattari 1987: 73.

11 Deleuze and Guattari 1987: 40; Jameson 1991: xxii.

12 Foucault 1977: 208.

13 Deleuze 1994: 129.

14 Deleuze 1994: 129.

15 Deleuze 1994: 130.

16 Deleuze 1995: 31.

17 Deleuze and Parnet 2007: ix.

18 Deleuze and Parnet 2007: 17–18 translation modified.

19 Deleuze 2006: 177.

20 Deleuze 2004: 278.

21 Deleuze 1995: 25.

22 This move was prefigured by Deleuze in his 1967 paper, 'The Method of Dramatization'. See Deleuze 2004: 106.

23 Deleuze 2006: 177.

24 Deleuze 2006: 179.

25 Deleuze 1995: 29. On the difference between science and philosophy see Deleuze and Guattari 1994: 127–9.

26 Deleuze and Guattari 1987: 333.

27 In an interview Deleuze mentions that he and Guattari were working on a cinema book, but somehow this didn't happen. Elsewhere he says he deliberately wanted to work on his own. See Buchanan 2008c.

28 Deleuze 1995: 32.

29 Deleuze and Guattari 1987: 6.

30 Deleuze and Guattari 1983: 43.

31 DeLanda 2006: 5–6.

32 DeLanda 2006: 40.

33 DeLanda 2006: 41.

34 Deleuze and Guattari 1983: 217.

35 For a more detailed account of this process see Buchanan 2008a: 88–116.

36 For a more detailed account of this argument see Buchanan 2011: 17–18.

37 Marcus and Saka 2006: 103.

38 Deleuze and Guattari 1983: 129.

39 For my critique of social sciences applications of the assemblage see Buchanan 2017a.

40 Phillips 2006: 108.

41 See also Alliez and Goffey's (2011: 10–11) discussion of the problems with 'assemblage' as a translation of agencement. In particular they note that it obscures the crucial implication that agencement concerns questions and issues relating to agency, which is obviously important.

42 Phillips 2006: 108.

43 Nail 2017: 22.

44 Law 2004: 41.

45 This is how Martin Joughin renders it in his translation of Deleuze's book *Negotiations*.

46 For example, *agencement* has also been translated as 'layout' and 'ensemble', both of which are too static in my view (see Guattari 1996: 160–4). Layout implies something much flatter and more fixed than an arrangement, which can at least imply a temporal as well as spatial aspect. The word 'ensemble' is similarly problematic because it lacks the contingency of arrangement, which can always fail. Assemblage is problematic for these reasons too, albeit much less so.

47 Laplanche and Pontalis 1973: 72–4.

48 Guattari 1995: 120.

49 Guattari 1995: 135. In the text Guattari actually refers to Julius Goldberg, but from the discussion that follows it is clear he meant Rube Goldberg.

50 Deleuze and Guattari 1994: 51.

Chapter 1

1 Browne 2003: 141. This is very far from the most disingenuous responses
   Darwin was to encounter. In later life, shortly before *On the Origin of the
   Species* was published, Philip Gosse published *Omphalos*, which argued that
   fossils were placed in rocks by God in order to create the impression that
   the earth had a longer history than it really had. Apparently, this was a step
   too far for most people and Gosse became a laughing stock. It is, however,
   a telling example of how far some people are willing to go in order to avoid
   changing their minds. See Hill 2019: 28.

2 Gould 2000: 276.

3 Deleuze 1994: 129.

4 Gould 2000: 24.

5 Gould 2000: 98–101.

6 Gould 2000: 25.

7 Gould 2000: 283.

8 Brookfield 2004: 115–16.

9 Gould 1987: 56.

10 For this reason, in my account of 'The Geology of Morals' I draw the
   opposite conclusion to both DeLanda (1997: 20) and Parikka (2015: 20).
   Rather than seek resemblances or points in common between geological
   formations and the structures of everyday life, I look instead at the way
   geology was founded as an academic discipline in order to solve problems
   that the examination of material elements alone could not resolve.

11 DeLanda 2016: 19.

12 Deleuze and Guattari 1987: 64.

13 Deleuze and Guattari 1987: 60.

14 DeLanda 2006: 28.

15 Deleuze and Guattari 1987: 57–8.

16 Deleuze and Guattari 1987: 59.

17 Deleuze and Guattari 1987: 62.

18 Deleuze and Guattari 1987: 61.

19 Hjelmslev 1961: 28.

20 Hjelmslev 1961: 29.

21 Hjelmslev 1961: 36.

22 Deleuze and Guattari 1987: 398–9.

23 Deleuze and Guattari 1987: 44.

24 Hjelmslev cited in Deleuze and Guattari 1987: 45.

25 Deleuze and Guattari 1987: 88.

26 Deleuze and Guattari 1987: 63.

27 Deleuze and Guattari 1987: 67.

28 Deleuze and Guattari 1987: 57.

29 Deleuze 1990: 170.

30 Deleuze and Guattari 1987: 40.

31 Deleuze and Guattari 1987: 69.

32 Deleuze and Guattari 1987: 40.

33 Deleuze and Guattari 1987: 327.

34 Deleuze and Guattari 1987: 45.

35 Deleuze and Guattari 1987: 62.

36 Deleuze and Guattari 1987: 62.

37 Deleuze and Guattari 1987: 62 (emphasis in original).

38 Deleuze and Guattari 1987: 43.

39 Deleuze and Guattari 1987: 44.

40 Deleuze and Guattari 1987: 50.

41 Deleuze and Guattari 1987: 70.

42 Deleuze and Guattari 1987: 71.

43 Deleuze and Guattari 1987: 73.

44 Deleuze and Guattari 1987: 91.

45 Deleuze and Guattari 1987: 100.

46 Deleuze and Guattari 1987: 194 (emphasis in original).

47 Deleuze and Guattari 1986: 87.

48 Deleuze and Guattari 1987: 168–9.

49 Deleuze 2001: 28. See also Buchanan 2006b.

50 Fitzgerald 1993: 72.

51 Deleuze and Guattari 1987: 76.

52 Cooper 2017: 81.

53 Deleuze and Guattari 1987: 159.

54 Deleuze and Guattari 1987: 161.

55 Deleuze and Guattari 1983: 29.

56 Deleuze and Guattari 1987: 269–70.

Chapter 2

1 See Svirsky 2012, 2014.

2 Bennett 2001: 180n37.

3 Deleuze and Guattari 1983: 26.

4 Deleuze and Guattari 1983: 25. See Kant 1929 (particularly Book II 'Analytic of Principles').

5 Deleuze and Guattari 1983: 310.

6 Deleuze and Guattari 1983: 25.

7 Deleuze and Guattari 1983: 27.

8 Deleuze and Guattari 1983: 129.

9 Deleuze and Guattari 1983: 129.

10 Deleuze and Guattari 1983: 129 (emphasis in original).

11 Deleuze 2006: 114.

12 Deleuze and Guattari 1987: 330.

13 Laplanche and Pontalis 1973: 65.

14 Deleuze and Guattari 1987: 399.

15 Deleuze and Guattari 1983: 26.

16 Deleuze 2006: 278.

17 Deleuze and Guattari 1983: 3.

18 Deleuze and Guattari 1983: 3. See also Guattari 1996: 210.

19 Deleuze and Guattari 1983: 37.

20 Bettelheim 1967: 235.

21 Bettelheim 1967: 243.

22 Deleuze and Guattari 1983: 37–8.

23 Deleuze and Guattari 1983: 37–8.

24 See Buchanan 2014.

25 Deleuze and Guattari 1983: 130.

26 Bennett 2001: 24.

27 Deleuze and Guattari 1987: 158.

28 There is a peculiar moment in *What is Philosophy?* where Deleuze and
    Guattari appear to collapse the plane of immanence and the abstract
    machine, which if it isn't a simple mistake on the authors' part must be
    counted as a significant departure from the original tertiary structure
    outlined in *A Thousand Plateaus*. Jeff Bell concludes from this passage
    that the abstract machine is the condition of possibility of the assemblage,
    but this seems wrong to me because it is the plane of immanence which
    exercises the power of selection and should therefore be accorded that
    status. However, if there is no distinction between the plane of immanence
    and the abstract machine then he is of course correct. To my mind the
    tertiary structure makes more sense than the implied binary structure
    found here, so I will continue to use that as my framework for thinking
    about the concept of the assemblage. But it is worth noting here that this
    kind of inconsistency is just one of the many reasons Deleuze and Guattari
    can be maddening. See Deleuze and Guattari 1994: 36 and Bell 2016: 66.

29 Bennett 2001: 24.

30 Deleuze and Guattari 1987: 77.

31 Bennett 2001: 31; Bhabha 1994: 203.

32 Bennett 2001: 31.

33 Deleuze and Guattari 1987: 82.

34 Deleuze and Guattari 1987: 86.

35 Deleuze and Guattari 1983: 44–5.

36 Klein cited by Deleuze and Guattari 1983: 45 (emphasis added by Deleuze and Guattari).

37 Deleuze and Guattari 1983: 46.

38 Deleuze and Guattari 1983: 47–8.

39 See Guattari 1984: 288. It is also worth noting that arrangement rather than assemblage is the preferred translation in this edition.

40 Deleuze and Guattari 1983: 44.

41 Deleuze and Guattari 1983: 44–5.

42 Deleuze and Guattari 1983: 47.

43 Deleuze 1989: 74.

44 Deleuze and Guattari 1986: 47.

45 For my discussion of this point see Buchanan 2016.

46 Deleuze and Guattari 1983: 9.

47 Deleuze and Guattari 1983: 9.

48 Deleuze and Guattari 1983: 9.

49 The set of letters 'a', 'b' and 't' can spell both 'bat' and 'tab', the content of both is the same, but the form differs. Moreover there is no direct correspondence between the content and its expression – 'b', 'a' and 't' does not map to heavy wooden object. See Hjelmslev 1970: 103.

50 Deleuze 1989: 74.

51 Deleuze and Guattari 1987: 142. See also Deleuze 1989: 16.

52 Deleuze and Guattari 1986: 85.

53 Deleuze 1989: 14.

54 Deleuze 1989: 132.

55 Deleuze 1989: 46.

56 Deleuze 1989: 45.

57 Deleuze 1989: 46.

58 Buchanan 2000: 15.

59 Deleuze 1989: 18. Two recent films exemplify perfectly this necessity to state everything in the Sadeian universe: *You and the Night* (Gonzalez 2013) and *Eva Braun* (Scafidi 2015).

60 For the same reason, as several commentators have pointed out, it is more important to campaign for justice than human rights because as recent pro-democracy protests have illustrated the law protects property and people first and does not concern itself with justice. It protects the people anti-fascists demonstrate against, not the demonstrators themselves, who are treated as criminals by the law. For a lucid account of the many inconsistencies in the relation between law and justice as it relates to pro-democracy demonstrations see Lennard 2019.

61 Deleuze 1989: 18–19.

62 Deleuze 1989: 20.

63 Deleuze 1989: 29.

64 Deleuze 1989: 19.

65 Deleuze 1989: 20.

66 Deleuze 1989: 41.

67 Deleuze 1989: 27.

68 Deleuze 1989: 27.

69 Deleuze 1989: 29.

70 Deleuze 1989: 31.

71 Deleuze 1989: 31.

72 Deleuze 1989: 71.

73 Deleuze 1989: 121.

74 Deleuze 1989: 71.

75 Deleuze 1989: 89.

76 Deleuze 1989: 119 (emphasis in original).

77 Deleuze 1989: 120 (emphasis added).

Chapter 3

1 Grosz 2008: 52.

2 Deleuze and Guattari 1994: 16.

3 Deleuze and Guattari 1994: 42.

4 Deleuze and Guattari 1987: 270.

5 Deleuze and Guattari 1983: 132.

6 Deleuze and Parnet 2007: 17.

7 Deleuze and Guattari 1987: 313.

8 Artaud 1976: 103.

9 Deleuze and Guattari 1987: 334. Lauren Berlant's concept of 'cruel optimism', defined as the situation in which 'something you desire is actually an obstacle to your flourishing' (2011: 1) is, in my view, a highly sophisticated analysis of this aspect of assemblages. This is not to say Berlant took the idea from Deleuze and Guattari, I hasten to add, but to suggest rather a confluence in their respective analyses of the world that I find illuminating.

10 As Deleuze and Guattari put it, we make love with our worlds.

11 Deleuze and Guattari 1987: 508–10.

12 Deleuze and Guattari 1987: 227.

13 Deleuze and Guattari 1987: 227.

14 Deleuze and Guattari 1987: 228.

15 Deleuze and Guattari 1987: 229.

16 Deleuze and Guattari 1987: 229.

17 Deleuze and Guattari 1987: 230.

18 Deleuze and Guattari 1987: 231.

19 Deleuze and Guattari 1987: 230.

20 Deleuze and Guattari 1983: 29.

21 Deleuze and Guattari 1987: 229.

22 I adapt this phrase from Lyotard 1993: 95.

23 Grossberg 2018: 139.

24 Deleuze and Guattari 1987: 315; Deleuze and Guattari 1994: 184.

25 For detailed accounts of Deleuze and Guattari's appropriation of Uexküll see Buchanan 2008a: 151–86; Gallope 2017: 225–8; Grosz 2008: 40–5.

26 Uexküll 2010 [1934]: 103.

27 Deleuze and Guattari 1987: 315–16.

28 Deleuze and Guattari 1987: 320. Anne Sauvagnargues similarly traces Deleuze and Guattari's interest in the territory and the refrain to a clinical source, namely Lacan's reinterpretation of Freud's grandson's so-called 'fort/da' game (which she misattributes to 'Little Hans'). See Sauvagnargues 2016: 128–9.

29 Deleuze and Guattari 1987: 332.

30 Deleuze and Guattari 1987: 317.

31 Deleuze and Guattari 1987: 311.

32 Deleuze and Guattari 1987: 314, 323.

33 Deleuze and Guattari 1987: 82.

34 Deleuze and Guattari 1987: 82.

35 Deleuze and Guattari 1987: 81.

36 Deleuze and Guattari 1987: 81.

37 Deleuze and Guattari 1987: 86.

38 Deleuze and Guattari 1987: 86.

39 Deleuze and Guattari 1987: 106.

40 Deleuze and Guattari 1987: 79.

41 Deleuze and Guattari 1987: 111.

42 Deleuze and Guattari 1987: 76.

43 Deleuze and Guattari 1987: 77.

44 Deleuze and Guattari 1987: 79–80.

45 Deleuze and Guattari 1987: 84.

46 Deleuze and Guattari 1987: 80.

47 Deleuze and Guattari 1987: 84.

48 Deleuze and Guattari 1987: 79.

49 Deleuze and Guattari 1987: 85–6.

50 Deleuze and Guattari 1987: 319–20.

51 Deleuze and Guattari 1987: 320.

52 Deleuze and Guattari 1987: 320.

53 Deleuze and Guattari 1987: 322.

54 Grosz 2008: 20.

55 Deleuze and Guattari 1987: 317.

56 Deleuze and Guattari 1987: 317.

57 Deleuze 1991: 1–2.

58 Deleuze and Guattari 1987: 318.

59 Deleuze and Guattari 1987: 318.

60 Turner 1969: 95–6.

61 Deleuze and Guattari 1987: 322.

62 Deleuze and Parnet 2007: 4.

63 Deleuze and Parnet 2007: 5.

Chapter 4

1 This chapter contains elements (in revised form) that were previously published in Buchanan 2017a.

2 Bennett 2010: 23.

3 Bennett 2010: 24.

4 Bennett 2010: 35.

5 Bennett 2010: 35.

6 Jameson 1990: 68.

7 Buchanan 2014.

8 Bennett 2010: 31.

9 Bennett 2010: 32.

10 Bennett 2010: 33.

11 Bennett 2010: 34.

12 Bennett 2010: 37.

13 Bennett 2010: 37 (emphasis in original).

14 Bennett 2010: 36.

15 Bennett 2010: 28.

16 Bennett 2010: 29.

17 Michaux cited in Deleuze and Guattari 1983: 6–7.

18 Bennett 2010: 37.

19 Jameson 1972: 123–9.

20 Lea 2014: np.

21 Lea 2014: np.

22 DeLanda 2006: 85.

23 Deleuze 1994: 131.

24 Lea 2014: np.

25 Deleuze and Guattari 1987: 67.

26 Lea 2014: np.

27 Lea and Pholeros 2010: 187–190.

28 Deleuze and Guattari 1987: 43–5.

29 Deleuze and Guattari 1987: 66.

30 Wacquant 2009: xvi.

31 This is why Wacquant describes the public debates about security and
    delinquency (form of expression) as a form of pornography – it 'transmutes
    the fight against crime into a titillating bureaucratic-journalistic theatre that
    simultaneously appeases and feeds the fantasies of order of the electorate,
    reasserts the authority of the state through its virile language and mimics,
    and erects the prison as the ultimate rampart against the disorders which [...]
    are alleged to threaten the very foundations of society.' Wacquant 2009: xiii.

32 Wacquant 2009: 6.

33 Wacquant 2009: 114.

34 Wacquant 2009: 61.

35 Wacquant 2009: 113.

36 Wacquant 2009: xxi.

37 Wacquant 2009: 80.

Chapter 5

1 The latter may have been the theme of his last published piece, but we don't
   know when it was written, and it seems rather sterile compared to the
   control society paper, which clearly opens out into a big new project. See
   Buchanan 2006b.

2 Deleuze 1995: 182.

3 Jameson 1994: 55–6.

4 Klein 2016.

5 This debate mirrors the way certain critics resisted the concepts of
   postmodernism and postcolonialism. As Jameson argued with regards to
   postmodernism, what we are witnessing now is the emergence of a new
   dominant form, not the instant extinction of the old form. Modernist works
   and ideas are still with us and still being produced, but they no longer have
   the cachet they once did, and they no longer define the 'cutting edge' of

artistic production as they once did. I discuss this in more detail in Chapter 3.

6 That there are no implicit moral or ethical limits to the lengths data companies will go in pursuit of profit can be demonstrated in any number of ways, so I will just offer one particularly egregious example of a drug company, Mundipharma, using Google searches to identify possible opioid users suffering from constipation by tracking their searches and then sending them targeted ads for their laxative laced product. See https://www.abc.net.au/news/2019-07-13/searches-data-mined-by-pharma-giant-to-promote-new-opioid/11300396 (accessed 14/07/2019).

7 Collini 2018: 35.

8 Jameson 1991: ix.

9 Zuboff 2019 (emphasis added).

10 Zuboff 2019.

11 See https://www.theguardian.com/technology/2014/oct/02/facebook-sorry-secret-psychological-experiment-users (accessed 14/07/2019).

12 https://www.abc.net.au/news/2019-07-13/facebook-5-billion-dollar-fine-cambridge-analytica-privacy/11306324 (accessed 14/07/2019).

13 Lanchester 2017: 3 (emphasis added).

14 Deleuze 1995: 179.

15 Deleuze 1995: 179.

16 Deleuze 1995: 181.

17 Deleuze 1995: 175.

18 Deleuze 1995: 180.

19 Deleuze and Guattari 1983: 236.

20 See Buchanan 2017b.

21 Zuboff 2019 (emphasis added).

22 Deleuze and Guattari 1987: 457.

23 Deleuze and Guattari 1987: 458.

24 Deleuze 1995: 178.

Bibliography

Alliez, E. and Goffey, A. (2011) 'Introduction', in E. Alliez and A. Goffey (eds), *The Guattari Effect*, London: Continuum, pp. 8–14.

Anderson, B. (1983) *Imagined Communities*, London: Verso.

Artaud, A. (1976) *Selected Writings*, ed. S. Sontag, Berkeley: University of California Press.

Bell, J. (2016) *Deleuze and Guattari's What is Philosophy? A Critical Introduction and Guide*, Edinburgh: Edinburgh University Press.

Bennett, J. (2001) *The Enchantment of Modern Life: Attachments, Crossings, and Ethics*, Princeton, NJ: Princeton University Press.

Bennett, J. (2010) *Vibrant Matter: A Political Ecology of Things*, Durham, NC: Duke University Press.

Berlant, L. (2011) *Cruel Optimism*, Durham, NC: Duke University Press.

Bettelheim, B. (1967) *The Empty Fortress: Infantile Autism and the Birth of the Self*, New York: The Free Press.

Bhabha, J. (1994) *The Location of Culture*, London: Routledge.

Brookfield, M. (2004) *Principles of Stratigraphy*, Oxford: Blackwell Press.

Browne, J. (2003) *Charles Darwin Voyaging*, London: Pimlico.

Buchanan, B. (2008a) *Onto-Ethologies: The Animal Environments of Uexküll, Heidegger, Merleau-Ponty, and Deleuze*, New York: SUNY Press.

Buchanan, I. (2000) *Deleuzism: A Metacommentary*, Edinburgh: Edinburgh University Press.

Buchanan, I. (2006a) *Fredric Jameson: Live Theory*, London: Continuum.

Buchanan, I. (2006b) 'Deleuze's "Life" Sentences', *Polygraph*, 18: 129–47.

Buchanan, I. (2008b) *Deleuze and Guattari's Anti-Oedipus*, London: Continuum.

Buchanan, I. (2008c) 'Five Theses of Actually Existing Schizoanalysis', in Buchanan and MacCormack (eds) *Deleuze and the Schizoanalysis and Cinema*, London: Continuum, pp 1–14.

Buchanan, I. (2011) 'Deleuze and Ethics', *Deleuze Studies*, 5 (4): 7–20.

Buchanan, I. (2013) 'Little Hans Assemblage', *Visual Arts Research*, 40: 9–17.

Buchanan, I. (2014) 'Schizoanalytic Modernism: The Case of Antonin Artaud', in P. Ardoin, L. Mattison and S. Gontarski (eds), *Understanding Deleuze, Understanding Modernism*, London: Bloomsbury, pp. 196–206.

Buchanan, I. (2015) 'Assemblage Theory and its Discontents', *Deleuze Studies*, 9 (3): 382–92.

Buchanan, I. (2016) 'What must we do about Rubbish?', *Drain Magazine*, 13: 1. http://drainmag.com/what-must-we-do-about-rubbish/.

Buchanan, I. (2017a) 'Assemblage Theory, or, the Future of an Illusion', *Deleuze Studies*, 11 (3): 457–74.

Buchanan, I. (2017b) 'Fear of Boredom', in P. de Assiss and P. Giudici (eds), *The Dark Precursor: Deleuze and Artistic Research*, Leuven: Leuven University Press, pp. 471–80.

Collini, S. (2018) 'Kept Alive for Thirty Days', *London Review of Books*, 40 (21): 35–38.

Cooper, M. (2017) *Family Values: Between Neoliberalism and the New Social Conservativism*, New York: Zone Books.

DeLanda, M. (1997) *A Thousand Years of Nonlinear History*, New York: Zone Books.

DeLanda, M. (2006) *A New Philosophy of Society: Assemblage Theory and Social Complexity*, London: Continuum.

DeLanda, M. (2016) *Assemblage Theory*, Edinburgh: Edinburgh University Press.

Deleuze, G. (1989) *Masochism: Coldness and Cruelty*, trans. J. McNeil, New York: Zone Books.

Deleuze, G. (1990) *Logic of Sense*, trans. M. Lester, London: Athlone.

Deleuze, G. (1991) *Cinema 2: The Time-Image*, trans. H. Tomlinson and B. Habberjam, Minneapolis: University of Minnesota Press.

Deleuze, G. (1994) *Difference and Repetition*, trans. P. Patton, London: Athlone.

Deleuze, G. (1995) *Negotiations 1972–1990*, trans. M. Joughin, New York: Columbia University Press.

Deleuze, G. (2001) *Pure Immanence: Essays on A Life*, trans. A. Boyman, New York: Zone Books.

Deleuze, G. (2004) *Desert Islands and Other Texts 1953–1974*, trans. M. Taormina, New York: Semiotext(e).

Deleuze, G. (2006) *Two Regimes of Madness: Texts and Interviews 1975–1995*, trans. A. Hodges and M. Taormina, New York: Semiotext(e).

Deleuze, G. and Guattari, F. (1983) *Anti-Oedipus: Capitalism and Schizophrenia*, trans. R. Hurley, M. Seem and Helen R. Lane, Minneapolis: University of Minnesota Press.

Deleuze, G. and Guattari, F. (1986) *Kafka: Toward a Minor Literature*, trans. D. Polan, Minneapolis: University of Minnesota Press.

Deleuze, G. and Guattari, F. (1987) *A Thousand Plateaus: Capitalism and Schizophrenia*, trans. B. Massumi, Minneapolis: University of Minnesota Press.

Deleuze, G. and Guattari, F. (1994) *What is Philosophy?* trans. H. Tomlinson and G. Burchell, London: Verso.

Deleuze, G. and Parnet, C. (2007) *Dialogues II*, trans. H. Tomlinson and B. Habberjam, New York: Columbia University Press.

Fitzgerald, F. Scott (1993) *The Crack-Up*, New York: New Directions.

Foucault, M. (1972) *The Archaeology of Knowledge*, trans. A. M. Sheridan Smith, London: Tavistock.

Foucault, M. (1977) 'Intellectuals and Power', in M. Foucault (ed.), *Language, Counter-Memory, Practice: Selected Essays and Interviews*, trans. D. Bouchard and S. Simon, Ithaca: Cornell University Press, pp. 204–17.

Freud, S. (1985) *Penguin Freud Library Vol 12*, trans. J. Strachey, London: Penguin.

Gallope, M. (2017) *Deep Refrains: Music, Philosophy, and the Ineffable*, Chicago: Chicago University Press.

Gould, S. (1987) *Time's Arrow, Time's Cycle: Myth and Metaphor in the Discovery of Geological Time*, London: Pelican.

Gould, S. (2000) *Wonderful Life: The Burgess Shale and the Nature of History*, London: Vintage Books.

Grossberg, L. (2018) *Under the Cover of Chaos: Trump and the Battle of the American Right*, London: Pluto Press.

Grosz, E. (2008) *Chaos, Territory, Art: Deleuze and the Framing of the Earth*, New York: Columbia University Press.

Guattari, F. (1984) *Molecular Revolution: Psychiatry and Politics*, trans. R. Sheed, London: Penguin.

Guattari, F. (1995) 'Balancing-Sheet Program for Desiring Machines', in *Chaosophy*, trans. R. Hurley, New York: Semiotext(e), pp. 123–50.

Guattari, F. (1996) *The Guattari Reader*, ed. G. Genosko, Oxford: Blackwell.

Harvey, D. (1990) *The Condition of Postmodernity*, Oxford: Blackwell.

Hill, R. (2019) 'Small Special Points', *London Review of Books*, 41 (10): 27–8.

Hjelmslev, L. (1961) *Prolegomena to a Theory of Language*, trans. F. Whitfield, Madison: University of Wisconsin Press.

Hjelmslev, L. (1970) *Language: An Introduction*, trans. F. Whitfield, Madison: University of Wisconsin Press.

Jameson, F. (1972) *The Prison-House of Language*, Princeton: Princeton University Press.

Jameson, F. (1990) *Late Marxism: Adorno, or, The Persistence of the Dialectic*, London: Verso.

Jameson, F. (1991) *Postmodernism, or, The Cultural Logic of Late Capitalism*, London: Verso.

Jameson, F. (1994) *The Seeds of Time*, New York: Columbia University Press.

Jameson, F. (2007) *The Modernist Papers*, London: Verso.

Jameson, F. (2009) *Valences of the Dialectic*, London: Verso.

Kant, I. (1929) *Critique of Pure Reason*, trans. N. Kemp Smith, London: Macmillan.

Klein, N. (2016) 'It was the Democrat's Embrace of Neoliberalism that won it for Trump'. https://www.theguardian.com/commentisfree/2016/nov/09/r ise-of-the-davos-class-sealed-americas-fate (accessed 04/02/2020).

Lanchester, J. (2017). 'You are the Product', *London Review of Books*, 39 (16): 3–10.

Laplanche, J. and Pontalis, J.-B. 1973 *The Language of Psycho-Analysis*, trans. D. Nicholson-Smith, New York: Norton.

Latour, B. (1999) 'On recalling ANT', in J. Law and J. Hassard (eds), *Actor Network Theory and After*, Oxford: Blackwell Publishing, pp. 15–25.

Law, J. (2004) *After Method: Mess in Social Science Research*, London: Routledge.

Lea, T. (2014) '"From Little Things, Big Things Grow": The Unfurling of Wild Policy', *E-Flux #58*, http://www.e-flux.com/journal/58/61174/from-little-thin gs-big-things-grow-the-unfurling-of-wild-policy/

Lea, T. and Pholeros, P. (2010) 'This Is Not a Pipe: The Treacheries of Indigenous Housing', *Public Culture*, 22 (1): 187–209.

Lennard, N. (2019) *Being Numerous: Essays on Non-Fascist Life*, London: Verso.

Lyotard, J.-F. (1992) *The Postmodern Explained to Children: Correspondence 1982–1985*, trans. J. Pefanis and M. Thomas, Sydney: Power Institute of Fine Arts.

Lyotard, J.-F. (1993) *Libidinal Economy*, trans. I. Hamilton Grant, London: Athlone.

Marcus, G. and Saka, E. (2006) 'Assemblage', *Theory, Culture & Society*, 23 (2–3): 101–6.

Nail, T. (2017) 'What is an Assemblage?', *SubStance*, 46 (1): 21–37.

Parikka, J. (2015) *A Geology of Media*, Minneapolis: University if Minnesota Press.

Phillips. J. (2006) '*Agencement*/Assemblage', *Theory, Culture & Society*, 23 (2-3): 108–9.

Sauvagnargues, A. (2016) *Artmachines: Deleuze, Guattari, Simondon*, trans. S. Verderber and E. Holland, Edinburgh: Edinburgh University Press.

Svirsky, M. (2012) *Arab-Jewish Activism in Israel-Palestine*, London: Ashgate.

Svirsky, M. (2014) *After Israel: Towards Cultural Transformation*, London: Zed Books.

Turner, V. (1969) *The Ritual Process: Structure and Anti-Structure*, London: Transaction Publishers.

Uexküll, J. (2010 [1934]) *A Foray into the World of Animals*, trans. J. O'Neill, Minneapolis: University of Minnesota Press.

Wacquant, L. (2009) *Punishing the Poor: The Neoliberal Government of Social Insecurity*, Durham, NC: Duke University Press.

Webb, T. (2009) *Teacher Assemblage*, Rotterdam: Sense Publishers.

Zuboff, S. (2019) 'Ten questions for Shoshana Zuboff', *The Guardian*, January 20, https://www.theguardian.com/technology/2019/jan/20/shoshana-zuboff-age-of-surveillance-capitalism-google-facebook (accessed 30/1/2019).

Index